*All that is necessary*
*for the triumph of evil is that*
*good men do nothing.*

Edmund Burke (1729–1797)

hidden histories series

## Most recent titles in this series

*'Deaf Me Normal': Deaf South Africans Tell Their Life Stories*
Ruth Morgan (ed)

*The Corner People of Lady Selborne*
John Mojapelo

*I Listen, I Hear, I Grow: The Autobiography of Ramaphakela Hans Hlalethwa*
Ramaphakela Hans Hlalethwa

*Christianity and the Colonisation of South Africa, 1487-1883. A Documentary History, Vol I*
Charles Villa-Vicencio & Peter Grassow

*Christianity and the Modernisation of South Africa, 1867-1936. A Documentary History, Vol II*
John W. de Gruchy

*Between Empire and Revolution: A Life of Sidney Bunting, 1873-1936*
Allison Drew *(co-published with Pickering & Chatto Ltd)*

*Robben Island to Wall Street*
Gaby Magomola

*The ANC's Early Years: Nation, Class and Place in South Africa before 1940*
Peter Limb

*Under Protest: The Rise of Student Resistance at the University of Fort Hare*
Daniel Massey

*Because They Chose the Plan of God: The Story of the Bulhoek Massacre of 24 May 1921*
Robert Edgar

# 'To Serve and Protect'

## The Inkathagate Scandal

*As told to Laurence Piper by Brian Morrow*

hidden histories series

**Series editors:**
Johannes du Bruyn
Nicholas Southey
Russel Viljoen

Unisa Press
Pretoria

First edition, first impression

**ISBN 978-1-86888-605-0**

Published by Unisa Press

University of South Africa
P O Box 392, 0003 UNISA

Designers: Dawid Kahts & Marlé Oelofse
Editor: David Levey
Typesetting: Dawid Kahts & Marlé Oelofse
Indexer: Marlene Burger
Printer: BusinessPrint

Readers are advised that this is the account of one man and the views expressed by him are not necessarily shared by the publishers of this book. Where possible, sources were checked to determine the veracity of the account.

# Contents

*In loving memory of my father Bill Morrow*

*Howay the lad's*

# Acronyms

*ANC* (African National Congress) – the oldest and largest black political movement in South Africa.

*AZAPO* (Azanian People's Organisation) – black liberation movement in South Africa, which AZAPO preferred to call Azania, influenced by Black Consciousness ideas, and particularly active in the 1980s.

*Black Sash* – a non-violent white women's anti-apartheid resistance organisation founded in 1955 by Jean Sinclair.

*BSS* (Black Students Society) – a university-based organisation for black students. Often the focal point for anti-apartheid activity on South African university campuses.

*CODESA* (Convention for a Democratic South Africa) – the lengthy multi-racial and multi-party meetings which decided how democracy should start in South Africa.

*COSATU* (Congress of South African Trade Unions) – labour union formed in December 1985. In the forefront of the struggle against apartheid in the late 1980s and early 1990s. It supported the international call for sanctions and was instrumental in organising strike action aimed at undermining the National Party government.

*ECC* (End Conscription Campaign) – liberal white organisation opposed to the system of conscription in South Africa. All white males over the age of 17 had to serve either 2 years in the army or 4 years in the South African Police.

*IDASA* (Institute for a Democratic Alternative in South Africa) – founded by Frederick van Zyl Slabbert and Alex Boraine at the end of 1986 to help find an alternative to the politics of repression and to explore new ways of addressing polarisation between black and white South Africans.

*Inkatha* – a Zulu political party violently opposed to the ANC in the 1980s and 1990s. Originally a cultural movement led by Chief Mangosuthu Buthelezi.

*KGB* – Russian intelligence agency particularly notorious during the Cold War.

*MI5* – British Intelligence agency responsible for protecting the United Kingdom against threats to national security.

*MI6* – British intelligence agency. Responsible for gathering intelligence relevant to UK interests outside the United Kingdom.

*MK* (*Umkhonto we Sizwe* meaning Spear of the Nation) – armed wing of the ANC set up after the Sharpeville Massacre in March 1960.

*NP* (National Party) – the white, mainly Afrikaner political party which ruled South Africa from 1948 to 1994.

*NSF* (National Students Federation) – student body covertly funded by the South African government. Designed to rival and undermine the more popular National Union of South African Students who were at the forefront of white student opposition to apartheid.

*NUSAS* (National Union of South African Students) – university-based organisation that campaigned against government policies and oppression in the 1980s and early 1990s. Heavily penetrated by government intelligence agents.

*SACP* (South African Communist Party) – key ally of the ANC during the struggle of apartheid; banned along with the ANC after the Sharpeville Massacre.

*SADF* (South African Defence Force) – the South African army. Essentially whites-only with the majority of servicemen being white conscripts serving their compulsory two-year service.

*SANSCO* (South African National Students Congress) – black student university organization. It merged with NUSAS to form one non-racial student organisation, SASCO (South African Students Congress) after the unbanning of the ANC.

*SAP* (South African Police) – the police force in South Africa, which ran on paramilitary lines with close links to the South African military and other intelligence agencies.

*SB* (Security Branch) – abbreviated term for the security branch of the SAP that monitored anti-government activity during the apartheid era.

*SRC* (Students' Representative Council) – elected student bodies at South African universities. The SRC tended to be anti-apartheid and pro-democratic (particularly at the English-speaking universities) but heavily penetrated by government intelligence agents.

*TRC* (Truth and Reconciliation Commission) – a body set up to make public the crimes conducted by all sides during the apartheid era. Amnesty was granted to individuals who made full and honest declarations of their involvement. It was not popular with many but it did provide a clear picture of how callous and inhumane the government had been during the apartheid era.

*UDF* (United Democratic Front) – multi-racial organisation formed in the 1980s. Responsible for orchestrating internal opposition to apartheid while the ANC was banned.

*UDW* (University of Durban-Westville) – non-white (primarily Asian) university in the suburb of Westville, Durban. Extremely militant; constant undercurrent of unrest via protest rallies, mass action and boycotts, often led to violent clashes with the SAP.

*UND* (University of Natal, Durban) – the major university in the province, nominally multi-racial but in the 1980s and early 1990s whites made up more than 90 percent of the student population.

*UWUSA* (United Workers Union of South Africa) – black labour union rival to the ANC-affiliated COSATU. Covertly set up and funded by the government via Inkatha, it adopted a pro-capitalist, anti-sanctions stance with the aim of portraying to the world that not all Africans supported sanctions.

Acknowledgements

When Laurence Piper and I embarked on this journey, in what now seems like a lifetime ago, I don't think that either of us thought it would take until the year 2010 to see our project reach fruition. Special thanks to Laurence for the key role that he played in making this project a reality. I think that it's safe to say that the book would have remained unpublished without his contribution. Another essential player was Martin Challenor, my Manor Gardens junior school soccer coach, journalist and estate agent whose input and interest in this project over those years has been invaluable. My gratitude and admiration go to Carolyn McGibbon, the wife of Billy Paddock, for her detailed corroboration of the harrassment her family endured and the amazing grace and spirit in which she received my account. Apologies it took so long.

A heartfelt and belated thank you to David Beresford, whom I met all those years ago in a Soho pub, for his willingness to go public with the information. Much appreciated. In addition, I would like to thank all the individuals who played a role in corroborating the events outlined in the book.

A sincere thanks to everyone involved in the publication process at Unisa Press, too numerous to mention, for making the dream a reality. Hopefully the long wait will be worth it!

The reasons behind the publication of the book are many and varied but I would like to take the opportunity to express my admiration and respect for former President Nelson Mandela, a man who has been a source of inspiration for many years and someone that I voted for in 1994, after queuing for many hours at the South African Embassy in London. To my former colleagues in the South African Police, friends and family, I hope that, with the passing of time, many of you have come to respect and understand the values that I stood up for and the reasons for my actions.

Brian Morrow

# Foreword

In July 1991 the *Weekly Mail* newspaper, together with the *Guardian* newspaper in London, published evidence that the apartheid government of South Africa had secretly given funds to the Inkatha Freedom Party (IFP). More specifically, the secret police (known as the Special Branch or just SB) had covertly channelled R250 000 to the IFP, or Inkatha as it was known at the time, to pay for rallies in November 1989 and March 1990. To make matters worse, the March 1990 rally had sparked the 'seven day war' in Pietermaritzburg; a conflict between the IFP and African National Congress (ANC) which left 200 people dead and 20 000 displaced.[1]

These revelations profoundly impacted on South African politics at a crucial point in the negotiations regarding a post-apartheid constitution. While allegations of collusion between the white-only National Party (NP) government and the IFP had long existed, the Inkathagate scandal provided irrefutable proof. This event forced the government to apologise, and obliged President FW de Klerk to remove the key Ministers of Defence and of Safety and Security. Embarrassed by these revelations, De Klerk began the process of reining in the various forces fomenting violence.

More broadly, Inkathagate undermined the IFP's credibility as an independent player in negotiations, scotching its ambitions to be regarded as one of the 'big three' players alongside the government and the ANC. Perhaps most importantly, Inkathagate prompted the government and the ANC to return to negotiations at a time when talks had been suspended, as both sides began to appreciate the cost to human life if negotiations failed. This resumption marked the turning point in the balance of power between the NP government and the ANC, and probably brought about a more democratic South Africa sooner.

In order to understand the fallout from Inkathagate more fully, it helps one to be reminded of the political context in South Africa at that time…

## Apartheid and Inkatha

An Afrikaans word literally meaning 'separateness', 'apartheid' was the electoral platform of the NP in the 1948 election. An Afrikaner nationalist party, the NP nevertheless advanced Afrikaner interests within the existing frameworks of white power and privilege from the preceding era of segregation. Presented as a system in which all people were 'separate but equal', in reality apartheid involved the political, economic and social domination of over 80% of the population by the white minority.

This majority was further divided into three black races: African, the indigenous people who constitute the vast majority of the population; Indian, those descended from immigrant labourers introduced to Natal in 1860; and 'coloured', mostly those of 'mixed race' but including the San and Malay slaves brought to the Cape in the 18th century. Indeed, according to the Population Registration Act of 1950 coloureds were defined as those who were not white, Indian or African.

Politically, only whites could vote and hold real political or administrative office, with the partial exception of traditional authorities who were retained as local authorities in many rural areas, called 'bantustans' or later, 'homelands'. Popular black political organisations were banned in 1960, and most civil liberties were suspended, including the freedom of the press, assembly and peaceful protest.

Economically, all well-paying jobs and most property ownership were reserved for white South Africans, while most state jobs were given to Afrikaners. Most black South Africans, especially Africans, were relegated to the ranks of manual labour on farms, factories and mines. With trade unions also banned, workers possessed few rights and even less pay. One reason why the gold mines of South Africa are the deepest in the world, stretching two kilometres into the earth, is the low cost of labour that made the extraction of the low-grade ore still profitable.

Socially, the practices of white South Africans, especially Afrikaners, dominated the public realm, from the official languages of the state, to the culture presented in the national media and on the sports fields. In addition, apartheid included a complete segregation of the races spatially, with the best residential areas, beaches, restaurants and the like being reserved for whites only. Sexual relations and marriage across the racial lines were also outlawed.

The entire system was fervently and often brutally backed up by the security forces. In addition to the military (the South African Defence Force or SADF), and the police (the South African Police or SAP), a number of intelligence divisions existed. These included: the Security Branch (SB) of the SAP, responsible for security in the Republic and the neighbouring states of Botswana, Lesotho and Swaziland; Military Intelligence (MI) of the SADF, responsible for Africa, especially the 'front-line' states of Angola, Mozambique, Zimbabwe, Zambia and Tanzania; and the National Intelligence Service (NIS), responsible for Europe and the rest of the world.

This was the context in which Inkatha was launched in 1974. Nominally a 'cultural-national' movement, led by Chief Mangosuthu Buthelezi, a member of the Zulu royal family, Inkatha was really a political movement launched after Buthelezi had consulted with the ANC. Formed in the province of Natal (which included the former Zulu kingdom) at a time when other anti-apartheid organisations such as the ANC were banned, Inkatha adopted the ANC colours and included many former ANC leaders, and grew quickly.

Notably, however, Inkatha tended to adopt a more conservative ideological and tactical stance than the ANC. This conservatism was partly due to the 'traditionalist' nature of its constituency and its leadership, but mainly because it was already immersed in the bantustan system of the 'Grand Apartheid' of Verwoerd, which co-opted traditional elites into a system of 'decentralised despotism'. Nominally, bantustans could become self-governing, but Pretoria retained the real powers, and also paid for the whole system.

Verwoerd's idea was to disguise real apartheid control behind a smokescreen of nominal 'national independence', presented as something akin to the 'winds of change' blowing colonialism away elsewhere in Africa. Inkatha's leadership justified its participation in Grand Apartheid, mostly in terms of pragmatic politics, by 'using the system from within' to press for change, especially in a context where militant resistance was, apparently, impossible. As it turned out, Inkatha's political judgement proved to be flawed.

## The demise of apartheid

By the 1980s apartheid was in crisis. On the one hand, the economy began to decline, spiralling into negative growth by the late 1980s. On the other hand, attempts at political reform by the National Party (such as the election of councillors in the black townships and the legalisation of trade unions) sparked a new and unprecedented wave of popular resistance openly aligned to the ANC. A wide range of student, civic, professional and issue-based organisations drew together to form the United Democratic Front in 1983. Further, in 1985 the recently legalised trade unions united to form the Congress of South African Trade Unions (COSATU).

Even before the formation of the UDF and COSATU, Inkatha and the ANC had publicly fallen out, ostensibly over ideological and tactical differences. Inkatha supported capitalism, the ANC less so; Inkatha rejected violence and sanctions to end apartheid, while the ANC endorsed them. In reality, the conflict centred on which organisation could claim to be the true leader of the oppressed in South Africa.

In this context, the surprise emergence of the flourishing militant organisations sympathetic with the ANC inside South Africa, suddenly posed a real and present danger to the status of Inkatha. Relations quickly degenerated when, following the ANC's lead, the UDF and COSATU painted Inkatha as an apartheid-friendly organisation whose leaders were complicit in the oppression and exploitation of black South Africans.

Virtually from the outset, Inkatha and the UDF/COSATU were political rivals, and before long this rivalry descended into violence. This conflict was covertly aided and abetted by the security forces which often intervened on the side of Inkatha. Given that internal security was the responsibility of the Security Branch, this unit was most often associated with both the oppression of the UDF/COSATU and the assistance of Inkatha. Indeed, in 1981 a special 'counter-insurgency unit' was established at Vlakplaas, near Pretoria. Under Eugene de Kock, this effectively became a 'dirty tricks unit' responsible for the torture, murder and massacre of suspected 'terrorists'.

In 1989 the stubborn and defensive PW Botha suffered a stroke, and was replaced by the more urbane and pragmatic FW de Klerk. Unbeknown to almost everyone, the end of apartheid was nigh.

## The transition to democracy

On 2 February 1990, State President FW de Klerk surprised all by unbanning the ANC and other organisations, and so inaugurated negotiations to end apartheid. In the following euphoric months, Nelson Mandela was released from prison; exiled ANC leaders began returning to South Africa; and the ANC and the South African government formally met and committed themselves to peaceful negotiations. In this context, Inkatha formally altered itself from a black-only political movement to a non-racial political party called the Inkatha Freedom Party (IFP).

Within a year of commencement, negotiations had stalled. At the heart of the problem were conflicting visions of the appropriate outcome and process of negotiations. The ANC wanted a centralised state governed by the majority, and rejected power-sharing along racial or ethnic lines. It viewed negotiations as a rapid process between itself, as champion of the oppressed, and the NP, as representing the oppressors, leading to an interim government that would oversee elections for a constituent assembly convened in order to decide the constitution.

In contrast, the NP envisaged a future constitution based on power-sharing for the various ethnic and racial groups in South Africa. Moreover, against the ANC's 'square table' vision of the negotiation process, which imagined only two participants negotiating, the NP representing the apartheid regime and the ANC presenting the oppressed, the NP embraced a 'round table' alternative. The latter amounted to a slow negotiation process inclusive of many parties and driven by bargaining and consensus, amongst existing institutions. This kind of process would effectively allow minorities to exercise powers of veto, enabling De Klerk to maintain white support. Negotiating amongst existing institutions meant that the NP would be well placed to influence events. Lastly, the transfer of power was to be followed by a process of shared governance for at least ten years.

Notably, the vision of the IFP was closer to that of the NP. It wanted a federal constitution, but also with real protections for minorities. It envisaged a negotiation process similar to that of the NP, but, at least, required that the IFP be recognised as part of a 'troika' along with the ANC and NP, necessary for any settlement. At heart, this reflected a desire for equal recognition alongside the ANC and NP.

The difficulties created by the conflicting visions were quickly and profoundly exacerbated by political violence that spiralled as 1990 progressed. While there had been violence between ANC-aligned organisations and the IFP in the province of Natal in the 1980s, the conflict now reached the heart of the country, the Witwatersrand, on an unprecedented scale.

In 1989 some 800 people were killed in KwaZulu-Natal, whereas in 1990 the death toll rose to 1500. In that same year more than 1000 people were killed in violence on the Witwatersrand, where violence polarised hostel dwellers, particularly migrant Zulu workers, who were invariably cast as being IFP, township dwellers who were cast as being members of the ANC.

For the NP, the continued existence of the ANC armed wing, *Umkhonto we Sizwe* (MK, 'Spear of the Nation'), was a major stumbling block, despite a secret meeting at D.F. Malan Airport in February 1991 where the ANC agreed that MK would be subject to the law of the land and would suspend all attacks.

For its part, the ANC had come to believe that the NP was deliberately using violence to bolster its position at the negotiating table. As Jeremy Cronin lamented, 'the government outwitted us during the first two years. While we talked with them on an élite level, they were fighting us on the ground with their "Double Agenda".'[2]

On 5 April 1991, the ANC publicly accused the security forces of complicity in the violence, demanding that the Ministers of Law and Order and of Defence be removed from office, the apartheid 'dirty tricks' units be disbanded, the police officers implicated in the violence be brought to justice, and the carrying of 'cultural weapons' by the IFP supporters be banned.

If these demands were not met, the ANC said, it would institute mass action as from 9 May. Both the NP and IFP denounced the tactics of the ANC, and De Klerk declared the creation of a special commission into the violence and a peace conference of national leaders. Late in April, the ANC dismissed such actions as being inadequate and withdrew from talks.

This was the context in which the Inkathagate scandal erupted, exposing vulnerabilities in the NP and IFP, and conversely boosting the ANC. Inkathagate sparked a series of revelations that, for the first time, irrefutably implicated the NP government in alleged political violence. It also revealed a degree of collaboration between, at a minimum, elements within the NP and IFP, although suspicions were widespread that such cooperation had reached the top leadership. Lastly, Inkathagate boosted the credibility of the ANC, an advance the party used to return to negotiations in a position of ascendancy.

## The National Party and violence

Inkathagate undermined the standing of the De Klerk government, especially abroad. For example, Japan, which was close to lifting sanctions in early August 1991, decided to wait for other countries to do so first. Spain announced that it would halt its push for the European Community to drop sanctions. The Commonwealth also suspended moves to lift sanctions.

In response, De Klerk tried to make amends. While denying his personal knowledge of the funding, his government officially confirmed that the payments and the source had been known to the Minister of Foreign Affairs, 'Pik' Botha; the Minister of Law and Order, Adriaan Vlok; the Minister of Defence, Magnus Malan; and Buthelezi's personal assistant MZ Khumalo. De Klerk demoted Adriaan Vlok and Magnus Malan, although they remained in his cabinet.

Until Inkathagate, the government had refused to grant an amnesty to 40 000 exiles, insisting that each apply individually for indemnity. It also refused to allow the United Nations High Commission for Refugees (UNHCR) access to returning exiles. In Geneva, on 16 August, the South African government and the UNHCR however agreed to an amnesty for all South Africans who had fled prior to 8 October 1990.

Unfortunately for De Klerk, these moves did not solve his problems. After the initial reports in the *Weekly Mail*, the National Party government claimed that the money was solely part of its anti-sanctions campaign, and added that all funding had been stopped in March 1990. However, as the scandal developed, the government was forced to admit to payments to other conservative groups both inside and outside South Africa, including the IFP's labour wing, the United Workers Union of South Africa (UWUSA)[3].

Further revelations concerning state collusion in political violence emerged over the following months. In late 1991 and early 1992 the National Party government once again found itself admitting to political conspiracy with the IFP when it acknowledged that the South African Defence Force (SADF) had trained some 200 Inkatha members in the Caprivi Strip in Namibia during September 1990.

Evidence of collaboration poured in thick and fast. In late 1991 former apartheid government secret agent Martin Dolinchek disclosed that the Bureau for State Security (BOSS), the forerunner of the NIS, had 'groomed' the IFP since its inception in 1974. According to Dolinchek the South African intelligence community and the CIA had cooperated in propping up the IFP. They established a rival organisation, Umkhonto kaShaka ('Shaka's Spear'), which was the brainchild of BOSS, and then deliberately discredited it in order to boost Inkatha and Buthelezi.

The *Weekly Mail* published further revelations based on information supplied by a former Inkatha official, Mbongeni Khumalo. Details of Military Intelligence front organisations being used to provide Inkatha money and training, were revealed. Amongst other activities, a camp was established at Mkhuze in Northern KwaZulu-Natal, where the Caprivi trainees were based before being absorbed into the police. The Goldstone Commission of Inquiry, charged with identifying causes of political violence, investigated the *Weekly Mail*'s allegations in 1992 and found that the SADF did train IFP members for offensive operations, but that the trainees did not constitute a death squad.

For the IFP, these embarrassing revelations were compounded by the second Goldstone Report, released the following month, which named IFP heavyweight Celani Mtethwa as a paid police informer during the 1980s, linked to apartheid death-squads commanded by Colonel Eugene de Kock, based at the Vlakplaas farm near Pretoria.

In 1996, a number of people, including former Minister of Defence Magnus Malan and MZ Khumalo of the IFP, were put on trial for the KwaMakhutha Massacre of 21 January 1987 in which 13 people, mostly women and children, were killed and several others injured. Daluxolo Luthuli, a former ANC cadre who had joined Inkatha in the late 1970s, submitted an affidavit that he was the commander of the Caprivi 200 who killed on the instructions of the IFP leadership. In 1994, Luthuli was involved with the mass militarisation of IFP supporters as part of the party's mobilisation against the 1994 election.

Although the accused were acquitted, the Supreme Court found that Inkatha members, trained by the SADF in the Caprivi, were responsible for the massacre at KwaMakhutha. The court also found that the two state witnesses, members of the SADF's Directorate of Special Tasks, were directly involved in the planning and execution of the operation. The court was not able to establish who had provided the backing for the attack.

Further revelations emerged from the Truth and Reconciliation Commission (TRC). Former security force personnel testified to protecting the IFP's Transvaal Youth Brigade leader, Themba Khoza, who became trapped in the grounds of the Sebokeng hostel after the massacre of 19 hostel inmates on the night of 3 September 1990. The commission heard that the local police had fabricated evidence to ensure that Khoza and the 137 IFP supporters arrested with him could not be linked to the firearms found in Khoza's vehicle and used in the massacre. According to Vlakplaas operatives, the weapons found matched those which they had provided to him the previous day. Further, Khoza's car was furnished by the Security Police.

Reflecting on the various submissions in 2000, the TRC found little evidence of a centrally-directed or formally constituted 'third force' fomenting violence during the negotiations. Nevertheless, it found that 'a network of security and ex-security force operatives, mainly acting in conjunction with right-wing elements and/or sectors of the IFP, was involved in actions that could be construed as fomenting violence.'[4] Thus for example, operatives from Vlakplaas systematically supplied arms to Inkatha in the Pretoria, Witwatersrand and Vereeniging (PWV) region.

## The IFP and collusion

In contrast to the government, IFP party leader Buthelezi denied personal knowledge of the Inkathagate scandal. Instead, his personal assistant, MZ Khumalo, took the blame, resigning from the party, only to be reinstated less than two years later in March 1993.

These machinations, plus Buthelezi's defensive and unrepentant handling of the matter on national television, severely undermined the IFP's credibility. Indeed, a major reason for the reluctance of the NP to engage the IFP after Inkathagate, was their concern regarding Buthelezi's increasingly maverick political style. This reputation was further tarnished by the subsequent revelations about the IFP's collusion in violence, as noted above.

Buthelezi was clearly very sensitive to the allegations that the IFP was some kind of government stooge, and I think it would be a mistake to believe that he was himself one. Indeed, even if it had been the case that collusion regarding violence between the IFP and NP went to the very top, the relationship was a strategic one between independent organisations.

To my mind, this is best illustrated in the confession by Vlakplaas boss Eugene de Kock that before handing over weapons to the IFP, Vlakplaas operatives tampered with these so that they would have a limited lifespan! At best, the relationship between the IFP and NP was an uneasy tactical alliance between two enemies of the ANC who fundamentally distrusted each other.

This claim is borne out by the dynamics of the negotiations. As already noted, the NP and IFP were natural allies in the negotiations arena, sharing very similar visions of a future constitution and the process to realise this. However, this alliance never really developed. On the one hand, the NP was ambivalent about the kind of relationship it desired with the IFP, while on the other, the IFP wanted recognition as an equal, not a junior, partner of the apartheid champion.

When negotiations began, the NP sought to consolidate the centre-right of the political spectrum, but appeared to be in two minds as to how to do so. While it sought to form relationships with parties like the IFP – indeed in 1990, rumours of an alliance abounded – it also opened its doors to all races in September 1990 and set about absorbing 'in-system' parties, such as the coloured Labour Party (LP).

These differences regarding tactics reflected deep divisions within the NP between those who favoured the IFP, usually the older, 'hawkish' NP leaders like Adriaan Vlok and Magnus Malan, and those who wanted to reach a concord with the ANC, usually the younger moderates such as Kobie Coetzee and Roelf Meyer.

The 'hawks' had the edge over the 'doves' for the first two years of the negotiations, but Inkathagate changed all that. After the revelations of July 1991, the NP was forced to adopt a new strategic tack and the moderates began to gain the upper hand. As a result, relations with the ANC improved, while those with the IFP deteriorated.

Since from the viewpoint of the IFP, and Buthelezi in particular, the key issue during negotiations was for them to be regarded as equal and necessary partners of any agreement, clearly this meant that the party could not become, or be perceived to be, an obedient ally of the National Party.

This position is consistent with Buthelezi's 'third-way politics' in the bantustan system – and later as regards Inkatha – where he attempted to walk the difficult road between the government and the ANC, a space deemed illegitimate by both the apartheid system and its major opponent. Buthelezi has always been his own man, albeit in ways perplexing to others.

In summary, it was not long before the IFP's desire for recognition, as an equal of the ANC and NP in the negotiation process, collided with the realities of exclusive ANC/NP deal-making. Frustrated at this marginalisation, the IFP increasingly turned to Zulu nationalist discourse and confrontational tactics, regularly storming out of negotiating forums and taking to the streets armed with 'cultural' weapons such as spears and *knobkerries* (wooden clubs).

## The ANC and the return to negotiations

For the ANC, the Inkathagate revelations seemed to bolster its claims that the IFP was a 'counter-revolutionary' force in the government's camp, as well as its specific allegation of the violent collusion between the government and IFP.

Thus, in its first public response to the scandal, the ANC argued that Inkathagate should be seen 'in the wider framework of a considered destabilisation policy by successive apartheid governments, including President De Klerk'. The party added, 'the "confession" of MZ Khumalo does not diminish the responsibility of the Inkatha leadership and Chief Buthelezi himself. We doubt that he could have been unaware of so generous a donation and its source'.

When breaking off negotiations a few months previously, the ANC had listed several conditions linked to political violence. Thanks to the revelations of Inkathagate, the NP government conceded to some of these, including the removal of Ministers Vlok and Malan from office, and the disbandment of 'death squads'. Furthermore, the scandal undermined the ability of the government to continue acting as a neutral 'guardian of the transition', enhancing ANC calls for a 'neutral referee' in the form of an interim government. In addition, De Klerk conceded that the SADF and SAP should become more accountable, thereby acknowledging the need to bargain.

Importantly however, although De Klerk's actions had not met all its conditions, the ANC decided to return to negotiations. The key reason here, as mentioned earlier, was a realisation by the leadership of the tremendous costs in terms of human life if negotiations failed. Indeed, the decision to return to negotiations by both sets of leaders was the path chosen despite the views of many of the ANC and NP rank-and-file.

Lastly, it was now apparent to all that negotiations meant agreement between the ANC and NP. They were the only parties necessary and sufficient for progress in bargaining. Regarding this issue, the IFP had failed, and the ANC's 'square table' vision of the negotiation process came to pass.

Consequently, over the next few months the pace of negotiations accelerated, taking the form of preparatory work for the National Peace Accord (NPA) set for September 1991. Although the NPA achieved little for peace, it did restore faith in a negotiated settlement, laying the foundations for the more substantial constitutional talks of the Conference for a Democratic South Africa (CODESA).

Interestingly, as the 300 NPA delegates gathered at the Carlton Hotel in Johannesburg, thousands of Inkatha 'warriors' staged mock battles in the streets outside, prompting a furious De Klerk to ask Buthelezi to disperse them. Symbolic of the IFP's increasing marginalisation from the NP and negotiation politics, and its virulent Zulu and confrontational reaction, this incident sums up the IFP's mind-set after the first two years of negotiations.

## Inkathagate and the new constitution

In retrospect, then, the Inkathagate scandal was good for negotiations, even while it was bad for the NP and especially so for the IFP. The scandal broke the deadlock caused by political violence, it began the process of reigning in the agitators of this violence, and it re-affirmed the dangers of a failure of negotiations for the leaders of the ANC and NP.

However, Inkathagate sparked more than just a return to negotiations. It was also a catalyst for the rise of moderates within the NP, a group more open to the ANC's conception of the negotiation process and its vision of a post-apartheid South Africa. While negotiations proceeded by fits and starts during the next two years, the basic dynamics that were established in the post-Inkathagate era remained constant throughout the remainder of the process.

Had Inkathagate not occurred, would the ANC and NP have returned to negotiations? Probably. However, one could equally probably assume that the return to negotiations would have taken longer, with a greater cost to human life, and with possible consequences for the character of the final constitution, had Inkathagate not taken place.

Imagine, for a moment, that the stand-off between the ANC and NP of early 1991 had lasted an additional six months or even a year. Surely many more lives would have been lost. Imagine, also, how popular attitudes would have hardened in this context, making the return to negotiations more difficult to justify. Imagine, too, how the balance of power between parties, and between hard-liners and moderates within parties, would have been affected. Imagine, now, the impact of the assassination of Chris Hani within this context.

In summary, it is not too much to say that the Inkathagate crisis of 1991 brought about the transition to a democratic South Africa sooner than would otherwise have been the case, at a lower cost to human life, and on terms preferred by the majority. Clearly then, the impact of Inkathagate extended much further than the firing of two cabinet ministers and the reversal of government policy regarding exiles.

## Inkathagate and Brian Morrow

This conclusion is all the more remarkable given the fact that Inkathagate was the work of one man, Brian Morrow, who at the time had been conscripted into the Security Branch of the South African Police in Durban. Outraged by the racism, corruption and torture rife in the SB, Brian resolved to do something to expose the reality of apartheid hidden from white South Africa and the world. Somewhat fortuitously, he stumbled across the Inkatha files and covertly copied them before fleeing the country and handing them to the media in 1991.

The fact that a security policeman exposed Inkathagate is remarkable enough. Even more remarkable is that he did so without financial compensation or public recognition. This is confirmed by Anton Harber, the Head of the School of Journalism at Wits University and, previously, editor of the *Weekly Mail*, who wrote 'Inkathagate… is one of the rare cases where the source had nothing to gain and everything to lose, but did it only out of good conscience'. Indeed, to this day Brian is unable to return freely to South Africa, having been refused amnesty from prosecution because his self-confessed theft of state documents had occurred after 1990, the cut-off date for amnesty applications.

This is one of the key reasons for this book. In addition, Brian wants to set the record straight on several accounts. Firstly, he claims that the media added nothing to the Inkathagate scandal that he had not provided to them. Indeed, in his view, their lack of effort possibly made it easier for some to claim ignorance of the funding. Brian insists this is a lie, and he gives evidence to support this claim. Furthermore, he contends that the network of CCB operations throughout South Africa was not properly exposed at the time, despite the leads he provided.

However, there is more to the Brian Morrow story than getting South African history right. Noteworthy is Brian's account of his cloak-and-dagger attempts to break the story in Britain, the various efforts by the apartheid security forces to stop him, including an alleged assassination, and the period during which he worked for MI6 before resuming something like a normal life as a teacher in Australia. To my mind, a remarkable feature of the Brian Morrow story is the human drama it portrays.

## Inkathagate: The book

I have never met Brian Morrow in person. Brian contacted me via email whilst I was in Toronto on sabbatical, for help in writing his story, and this book is the outcome of our work using email.

I must confess that initially, I was somewhat wary of Brian. After all, when he was in the 'White Organisations' section of the Security Branch, I was a student activist on the Howard College campus in the (white) National Union of South African Students (NUSAS). I was really bothered by the idea that someone could claim to be anti-apartheid and yet still end up in the security police, especially after having been to university where he would have been exposed to some of the real goings-on in the country.

At the same time however, I was impressed by what appeared to be Brian's selfless role in the Inkathagate scandal, and intrigued to find out the inside story about an important and under-appreciated event in South Africa's transition to democracy. So, after some reflection, I decided to engage Brian and see where the interaction led, but on the condition that I was not simply a ghost-writer, and that my status as an independent scholar was kept intact. To this end, I suggested that, in addition to writing the introduction, the body of the book would take a question and answer format so that our voices could be kept distinct. Brian was not enthusiastic about this idea, but agreed nevertheless.

We began in mid-2005 with Brian writing his account of what is now the chapter entitled 'thief' – the heart of the story really. I was amazed at the rate at which the words tumbled out of him. I was also amazed at the detail he managed to recall. I reflected, with embarrassment, on the vagueness of my own memories from the late 1980s. On receiving his email I read it and replied, and asking questions to fill gaps in the story or to obtain explanations for Brian's actions.

Brian replied a few days later, answering my queries, and this became the general pattern of our dialogue for each chapter. The only significant difference was that, in later edits, I would re-organise the structure of the chapter so that our 'conversation' made more sense. In short, while I helped edit, prompt and organise his text, what follows in this book is Brian's story, expressed in his own words.

Most of our work took this largely formal, almost technical, dialogical format. However, there were moments where substantive disagreements arose, for instance around the term 'thief' for chapter three. Brian was worried that this portrayed him in an immoral light when his actions were clearly intended to expose wrongdoing; I felt it added a sense of drama to his story and accentuated the extraordinary nature of his experiences. Over time Brian acquiesced and the chapter title remained.

There were also other times when Brian became frustrated with my scepticism towards him, but by the final version of the document, I had agreed to remove the question and answer format from the text. Partly, this reflected the recommendations of various readers, but the main reason was that I no longer feared myself to be the potential victim of some dissembler pursuing a hidden agenda, or a delusional product of post-traumatic stress disorder. After a year of correspondence with Brian, of checking his story with the people he named, and of consultation with friends and colleagues, I have come to the conclusion that Brian is quite as he presents himself: an ordinary person who found himself in extraordinary circumstances, and who through choices both good and bad, lived, and continues to live, an exceptional life.

In conclusion, I would like to thank the following for their help in confirming, and at times commenting on, Brian's story: Martin Challenor and Gary Cullen for aspects of Brian's childhood and varsity life; Carolyn McGibbon for confirming Brian's detailed account of the Security Branch harassment of Billy Paddock and herself; Graeme Jordan and Keith Marallich for confirming the activities of the Special Branch, and David Beresford and Anton Harber for authenticating Brian's account of the exposé.

I would also like to thank all the people who read and commented on the book, including Jason Arsenault, Nonhlanhla Chanza, Sherran Clarence, Jean Dyson, Jonathan Hyslop, Brian Khoza, Ilan Lax, Gerhard Maré, Penny McKenzie, David Moore, Sanele Nene and Piers Pigou.

A special thanks to Martin Challenor for facilitating many contacts, meetings and his general support. Without Martin, this book would be substantially poorer. Most of all though, I would like to thank Brian Morrow for trusting me as the midwife of his remarkable tale. With Brian's story, another piece of the history of the South African 'miracle' falls into place.

*Laurence Piper*

# 1

# Conscript

My adventures really began when I was conscripted into the Security Branch (SB) of the South African Police, but perhaps I should start with a quick sketch of my life prior to that.

I had as good an upbringing as anyone could wish for, particularly with regard to my parents who were simply fantastic. I was born in East London, in the Eastern Cape, in 1962 but moved to Durban at a very young age. We lived in the (white-only) suburb of Howardene, just behind the old University of Natal, Durban (UND) library, and my parents started a small drapery firm which, through hard work and entrepreneurship they transformed into a successful business.

My family, which included a brother, Norman, six years older, and a sister Beverley, three years older than I, pretty much lived the South African dream. Our house was certainly luxurious with five bedrooms, three bathrooms, four lounges and the obligatory pool.

We, in common with most white families, employed servants. However, I would argue that my parents' attitude was fairly enlightened by the standards of the time. For instance, we had only two 'maids' in a 17-year period between 1974 and 1991, in stark contrast to others in the area whose mistreatment of their servants forced them to look for new staff on a regular basis.

Our first maid, Idah, remains in contact with us to this day. I remember last seeing her on the day of my father's funeral in 1998. Idah and I bumped into each other at my mom's front gate as she arrived to pass on her condolences on my dad's death. We had not seen each other for years but our mutual pleasure at meeting again (for some reason I had always been the favourite and must admit that Idah spoilt me rotten) led to a massive hug. Well, it may have been 1998 but you should have seen the looks of the passersby! A white man hugging a black woman! I think I would have caused less fuss if I had run stark naked up the street!

Idah, and her successor Andrina, enjoyed privileges of which the majority of her contemporaries could only have dreamed at that time. In everything but name they were considered as part of the family. My parents turned a blind eye to Idah's partner staying over in her room, contrary to the Group Areas Act. They installed modern amenities in her living quarters; in fact Idah must have held the record for being the first servant with a television. They granted Idah days off, not common practice at the time, and of course, she ate what we ate, and boy, was she a good cook.

Various 'garden boys' ('boy' was effectively a derogatory term as the age of the gardener could be anything from 12 to 60), often relatives of local servants, also took a shine to me as I regularly joined in local soccer matches in the park, bringing Coke and Fanta from home for refreshment.

I'd have to say that my 'liberal' tendencies have their roots in my upbringing, most notably regarding my relationship with Idah, Andrina and my father. My mother used to regale guests with boring yet true stories of my regular walks back from South Beach – quite a long slog to Howardene I can assure you – because I used to give my bus fare to the African beggars on the way home. I think this identifies me as being both generous and stupid from an early age!

My early school life was idyllic, other than being white-only of course. I attended the local school and was certainly one of the 'in-crowd'. Being reasonably proficient at sport and attending the same school as most of your mates clearly had its advantages.

The good times came to a shuddering halt when my parents enrolled me at Durban High School (DHS) instead of my preference, Glenwood – the school all my friends attended. High school was endured rather than enjoyed but nevertheless, I established lifelong friendships, so it was not all a waste.

Life outside of school was good. I went on yearly trips to the UK with my dad, forging a close bond between us and fostering a life-long love of football and England. My father was born in Durham, in the north of England, and still had family there whom we visited. He was an ardent Newcastle United fan, and passed this on to me.

Exposure to the news and 'normal' life in the UK must also have played a part in my growing sense of uneasiness at the racial structure of South African society. Increasingly, I found my liberal views at odds with those of my friends and even my family, particularly those of my brother and sister.

As our matric year drew to a close, my friends and I, along with all the other white males of the same age were faced with a tough decision. Go straight to the army after school, or apply for deferment and head for university? My own choice was easy. Anything but the army for me. So off I went to the University of Natal, Durban campus (UND), with little other than a desire to stay out of the clutches of the SADF.

To say that I enjoyed my university years would be an understatement. I truly believe that I led the easiest life of any student, possibly in the world! Consider the evidence. My parents bought me a brand-new car for my 18th birthday: an Escort Sport complete with Petro Card for an unlimited fuel supply. This went well with my own personal Gold American Express card and a virtually unlimited supply of 'pocket money' from my parents. Oh, and of course my parents paid for all my tuition fees! No working in Maccas for this student!

University further opened my eyes to the inequalities of our society. This was highlighted by an incident that took place in Durban whilst I was completing a survey as part of a history assessment. I was assigned to work with two 'coloured' students whom I knew fairly well from our lectures. Having completed our assigned task in the Durban city centre, I suggested that we should have a quick bite to eat at a local restaurant. They both looked at me with a mixture of shock and amusement. 'Brian, we can't eat there. It's whites-only!'

I can remember feeling anger at the stupidity of it all. What a bloody setup! Friends couldn't just enjoy a meal in each others' company because of some arbitrary pigmentation differences!

As apartheid was so successful in keeping the races apart, these instances were fairly rare for whites. If they had happened more frequently then maybe people would have asked questions, but the government was nothing if not successful in keeping contact between the races restricted to a master/servant basis. Meeting blacks of a similar or superior standing was restricted at all costs.

Aside from such incidents, which usually led to a heated family debate at home, my life consisted of attending as many clubs, playing as much sport, and having as much fun as possible. Of course, as the years passed, the reality of conscription became unavoidable and my career in the police force became a reality.

I was often tempted to join anti-apartheid student organisations but lacked the courage of my convictions. I attended various anti-apartheid rallies on campus but never seriously considered standing for the anti-apartheid Students' Representative Council (SRC). There is no way of avoiding the fact that I took the easy way out, only venturing to express my opinions in personal conversations with friends or acquaintances.

From the outside, the SRC also seemed to be something of a closed shop. On the odd occasion when I summoned up the courage to get involved, I was invariably given the brush-off. The names of the various SRC members of the early 80s are now a bit of a blur, but David Ensor also went to DHS though we were never friends, as did Gary Cullen.[5]

### Comment: Gary Cullen

Brian perceived us [the SRC] as a closed shop and he was not alone in this. I, on the other hand, saw Brian (we were at the same school together, in lectures, and he grew up in the neighbourhood of my then girlfriend) as another conservative or apolitical white student who viewed us with scorn. So any perceived closedness would have been more a self-protective thing – very much like his own feelings…

By the way, when Brian Morrow worked for the SB he and I played in the same varsity social football side. At that time I had been told (not sure by whom) that he worked for them.

My friends, whilst fairly liberal, never questioned any aspect of the regime. Everyone that I knew completed their stint in the military and got on with their lives. At university, the most demanding issues were finding the next party and a girlfriend.

Perhaps fortuitously, I did not meet my wife, Michelle, at this time. She and I encountered each other some time later towards the end of my studies in 1985, at the Durban club at the Warehouse, a popular nightclub in those days.

Michelle was apolitical to the extreme, particularly in the mid-80s, and initially she found my political stance rather unique. It was nearing decision time for me because conscription loomed on the horizon. The development of my relationship with Michelle definitely tilted my final decision towards the police. Otherwise, I'm fairly certain that I would have headed for the UK and exile.

Every six months since my matric year, I had received conscription notices. The scheduled posting was always Five South African Infantry Battalion at Ladysmith, which was considered to be a virtual guarantee of being sent to Angola after the obligatory six months basic training.

As it was, I never contemplated conscription into the SADF (South African Defence Force). That was an absolute non-starter. There was no way in the world that I was going to enforce apartheid on the National Party's (NP) behalf! However, I had always considered the SAP (South African Police) to be a viable alternative. I figured that I might be able to do some good working from the inside, so to speak, and of course it never crossed my mind that I would end up in the notorious Security Branch. I imagined myself working in a local charge-office dealing with breaches of criminal law rather than enforcing apartheid.

In addition, I felt that in the SAP, I could resign if things didn't work out as planned, whereas in the SADF I would have faced criminal prosecution if I deserted.

If I had not been engaged at the time I would certainly have sought political asylum in the UK as this had long been my preferred option, but Michelle was not ready to leave her family. Basically I placed my personal feelings before my conscience.

However, my entry into the police force, like so many other areas of my life, did not run smoothly. Fate had other ideas. After passing through all the basic police selection procedures I failed my eye test. I was out! Time was not on my side as I was due to begin basic training at Five Infantry Brigade in Ladysmith in January 1986!

The atmosphere was tense at home. Although the issue was never raised, my parents knew that I would not be joining the army. I think they lived in the constant fear that I might join the ANC or become a conscientious objector! Although he did not share my political views, my brother never hassled me over my beliefs, but my sister felt that I was 'being a wimp' and worrying my parents unnecessarily. According to her, 'everyone else went to the army without making a big fuss about it!'

A friend from varsity came up with a solution – join the Railway Police! He had read that the Railway Police were going to amalgamate with the SAP in the near future and this would be a good way to solve my dilemma. Now, I must admit I took a bit of convincing as the Railway Police had such a bad image. There were seen as probably even more reactionary and racist than the SAP. Plus they wore an ugly green uniform!

Anyhow, I saw the logic behind the move and somewhat reluctantly applied for enlistment. Once more I sailed through the selection procedures until the time came for the dreaded eye test. This time I decided to cheat!

I bought brand-new contact lenses, omitted to tell them that I wore either glasses or lenses and passed the examination. I was in! Oh joy of joys! I was assigned to Durban Central Railway Station, having never travelled on a South African train or even walked into a railway station in my life.

Having led a privileged existence up to this point, just working for a living was a new experience. The Railway Police opened up a whole new world. I never realised how many Afrikaners lived in Durban. There was an entire sub-culture out there that I wasn't aware of. Up to this point, my world-view had been dominated by white English-speaking South Africans.

Initially, I was posted to carry out charge-office duties (in plain clothes because I was not yet qualified). This was quite an achievement in itself since probationer student constables usually found themselves locked away in the confines of the radio room until after their basic training. Being the lone Englishman made me rare, but being in possession of some educational qualifications sent me into the social stratosphere! I have to confess that I led a somewhat charmed existence during my time at Durban Central, thanks to my unique identity.

Central to being a Railway Policeman was being a racist. On my first day I learnt several new racist words. Of course I had heard the word '*kaffir*'[6] before, but never in my own house, and certainly never from my lips. Here it turned up in virtually every sentence. And of course, if it wasn't '*kaffir*' it was '*houtkop*' (wooden head), a completely new one to me, but something I was to hear a lot of during the coming years. It was clear from day one that blacks were simply not seen as being fully human.

On day two I saw racism in practice on an unprecedented level. A call came out for a stretcher and blankets to be taken up to one of the platforms as a black civilian had been killed whilst attempting to board a moving train. Apparently it was the last train out to KwaMashu for the evening, and I can recall wondering why anyone would take such a risk. Later, having seen how some Railway Police types passed the time on nightshift, the dead man's actions made more sense.

On our arrival at the scene, we saw that the victim had been decapitated. He had been caught by the rear wheels of the last carriage, having failed in his desperate attempt to leap onto the stairway. This was my first experience of death.

Strangely, I was not that affected by the body. Far more shocking and repulsive were the attitudes of my 'colleagues'. Their complete lack of compassion for the deceased shocked me. Things got worse when the decapitated head was picked up by the ear and then fell on the ground as the skin came away in the carrier's hand. One of the group shouted 'anyone for a *braaivleis* (barbecue)?'

Once we had carried the corpse up to the upper level to await the arrival of the mortuary van, some policeman took great delight in showing passing blacks the grisly remains! It was all so alien that I just didn't know how to deal with it.

Racism was widespread and the force was large. I remember being amazed by the size of the police contingent at Durban Central Railway Station. Given how busy the place was, I soon realised that a permanent police presence was warranted.

It did not take long to come to my attention that torture was considered to be a standard interrogation technique, although it lacked the precision and meticulousness I was to encounter in later years. Here, it was more of a quick beating in one of the cells or offices with passers-by pretending not to hear the moans and groans coming from behind the closed doors.

A number of the constables with whom I worked displayed an attitude towards blacks that verged on psychopathic hatred. To this end, they considered administering the odd beating to blacks waiting for trains, or homeless vagrants seeking some form of shelter, as part of their everyday duties – especially while on night shift.

On one occasion, a particularly racist individual, a constable carried out a vicious attack on an illegal hawker in the central station, raining down blows and kicks on her defenceless body whilst a group of fellow officers looked on. I could turn a blind eye to some things that I didn't have the power to alter, but not this. I yelled at him to stop but he ignored me, so I intervened physically.

At that stage, I was heavily into my gym and was fortunate to be one of the stronger members of the force. He certainly was no match for me, particularly given the rage his actions had aroused. Despite mumblings from some colleagues about me being a '*kaffirboetie*' (*kaffir* brother), no one really supported him and he went on his way without reporting my actions.

It really came as no surprise a few years later when I heard that he had been killed in an altercation with a group of blacks, whilst of duty. I'm sure someone either passed a comment or looked at his woman in a manner that his racist mind couldn't cope with and he started something that he couldn't finish.

As time passed, I fell out with a number of senior members at Durban Central, mostly low-level sergeants and warrant officers. Basically, we just rubbed each other up the wrong way. I considered them to be geriatric racist dinosaurs and they presumably felt that I was a know-it-all *soutpiel*[7] and young-to-boot. Where I could, I stood up for blacks and the occasional whites who were arrested and maltreated. I just developed a reputation, I suppose.

My hide was saved on a number of occasions by a Lieutenant Bala Naidoo who has gone on to some success as SAPS Media Relations Officer for KwaZulu-Natal, reaching the rank of director. He intervened on my behalf by arranging a transfer to the train mobile-unit after an altercation with a duty sergeant regarding a duty-roster allocation.

I was really lucky because the job was interesting, although the logic behind the transfer was somewhat strange since I had no training whatsoever. Anyhow, my new assignment was exactly the type of policing that I had hoped to do. Our task was to travel on trains – ostensibly incognito, but our white skins gave us away – and protect commuters.

Travelling by train was not a pleasant experience for the average black person. Gangs of armed youths would circulate through the carriages demanding money. If you failed to comply, they had a habit of throwing you out of the moving train. Our job was to seek out such gangs, whilst searching for contraband weapons and drugs.

I have to say it was without doubt my most rewarding time in the force. On the whole, my colleagues were honest, less racist than any others I encountered, and dedicated to their work.

One incident highlighted the twisted nature of policing under apartheid. Whilst on patrol with my partner (we often used unmarked four-wheel drive cars to move between various stations, although we had limited legal jurisdiction outside of Railway property), we received a call over the radio that a black civilian had been thrown from a train in the vicinity of the Umgeni Road station.

We made our way to the scene and started looking for the victim. After scanning the open train-track we heard groans coming from a nearby train tunnel. This meant that the victim was more than likely on the tracks in the tunnel. What the hell did we do now? We radioed a request that the line be closed so that we could provide assistance to an injured victim. This request was denied! Again, had it been a white person, the line would have been closed. Such was life under apartheid!

Anyhow, this response left us in a dilemma. We felt that we had to help but were both extremely concerned that a train might hit us while we were in the tunnel. Also, how on earth were we to assess the victim's injuries in the blackness of the tunnel?

We decided to make the best of a bad job. Collecting our stretcher and first-aid kit we headed off into the darkness. It seemed like eternity at the time but it wasn't too long before we located the accident victim and eased him onto the stretcher. There was no way we could assess the extent of his injuries given the circumstances. We simply worked on the principle that anything would be an improvement on his present situation. Sweating profusely with anxiety, we made off as quickly as possible, carrying our injured casualty. Luckily no train came along to kill the three of us.

After exiting the tunnel, we headed for the King Edward Hospital. Of course, on the way to King Edward we passed numerous other hospitals that could have provided much quicker assistance but, unfortunately, in 1986 they were for whites only. What was that about 'separate but equal'?

Upon arrival at the casualty department, I came face to face with a 'Heart of Darkness' vision that took my breath away. I had never visited a black hospital before. It was appalling! Patients lay strewn across the floor of the waiting room, taking up every available space. Blood was spattered across the entire area. It was a Friday night, apparently a popular time for 'faction-fighting' and robbery, but this was all new to me.

One particular sight will remain in my memory for all time. There, amid all the chaos sat a man, lucky enough to have a seat, but with an axe imbedded in his skull, calmly waiting for his turn to see a doctor. What a bloody country!

The other major event of my time in the Railway Police was my first intelligence job. For some reason, the senior staff officers continued to value my input and presence, despite my growing reputation as a 'liberal'. In July 1986 a senior officer asked if there was any way that I could attend a UDF rally at Curries Fountain Soccer Stadium with a view to submitting a report on the event. This protest was to be held on the same day as the inaugural launch of the United Workers Union of South Africa (UWUSA) at Kings Park, an event that was to take on more significance in years to come.

People might argue that I could have turned down the request, but I was genuinely interested and thought it might be quite enlightening, so I did not. I still had 'liberal' friends on campus who were planning to attend and so it wasn't difficult to obtain an 'invite' to the demonstration. I never advertised my employment outside of my close circle of friends so these acquaintances were not aware that I was a policeman.

It was, however, a fairly surreal experience as I observed, and to some extent shared, their fearful/excited response to passing SAP Casspirs and hovering helicopters. Not to mention the obligatory video squad who carefully collected footage of the 'communist agitators'. Hello Big Brother!

Having listened to the speeches, and collected enough literature to start my own library, I made my way back to headquarters. Although nothing significant happened on this trip, it was one of the scariest of my life. Imagine the scene. A solitary white male adorned with UDF stickers and associated anti-apartheid paraphernalia in a train jam-packed with black commuters, many with strong Inkatha links.

I received some very strange looks on that journey, I can tell you. My fingers never left the butt of my dad's 6.35 Bernadelli pistol that I had 'borrowed' for the day! It would have been futile but it made me feel a whole lot better.

This incident illustrates the lack of planning and amateurism that was prevalent at the time. I could easily have been picked up somewhere safer, but no one thought of that. I submitted my report, received the kudos for my bravery and cooperation and everyone was happy. I presume the SAR (South African Railways) top brass simply wanted to show the SAP that they had access to 'sources' and 'intel' even though I'm sure they wouldn't have wanted the Security Branch (SB) to know how they had obtained it.

On the amalgamation of the SAR Police into the SAP I headed off for basic training at the white Police College in Pretoria in January 1987. At that time each racial group had their own training facility. Blacks trained at Hammanskraal in the Transvaal, coloureds at Lavis Bay near Cape Town and Indians at Wentworth in Durban. Since I possessed a degree, I would complete a short course of approximately three months while the rest of the intake undertook the regular six-month tour.

Pretoria Police College is a huge facility. At that time it catered for upwards of 2500 (all white) cadets per intake. Our platoon (54 Platoon) consisted of 30 male and four female cadet constables. All the members of the platoon had either to hold a degree or to have served in a full-time capacity in another branch of the state military apparatus. The girls joined us after breakfast because, obviously, they were housed in a separate facility.

As pleased as I was to be included in the short-course intake, I have to confess that at the time, I considered basic training to be hell on earth. As usual I started off on the wrong foot, so to speak, by fracturing my right hand in a fall just prior to going to college. I gritted my teeth for the first few weeks but eventually I was sent to a specialist who placed my arm in a plaster cast.

To a civilian who hasn't endured basic training, our daily instruction would seem harsh, if not somewhat senseless, but I have to confess that we were vastly better off than the other recruits at the college. Our day would begin sometime between 03h00 and 03h30 when the entire squad would prepare the dormitory for the mandatory 05h00 daily inspections by Sergeant Rothman and Warrant Officer Kluyts.

Everyone was required to clean their own personal area and ensure that their bed was made. Now this may sound easy enough but there could not be one speck of dust and the bed had to be flat with the corners at 90 degrees. Most cadets followed the time-honoured practice of sleeping on the floor during the week, thereby only having to construct the 'perfect bed' once a week! Not so good for the back though and rather cold in early autumn and winter.

The walls and floor next to the bed had to be painstakingly polished each day and all uniforms precisely folded in the locker. Your R1 rifle had to be neatly disassembled on the bed in mint condition. The ablution block had to be cleaned, although we reduced our workload by voting to not use the urinals and everyone showered at night.

The cadets had selected Daantjie Conradie, an ex-prison lieutenant, as our platoon leader and subsequent events proved our choice to be a wise one. Due in no small part to his high standards, 54 Platoon never failed an inspection. This was no mean achievement and quite a bonus as it provided us with a much needed hour or so of rest before the start of the day.

Those who failed inspection had to endure some form of physical punishment in order to learn the error of their ways via the '*opfok*' (literally 'fuck up'). This usually took the form of a run while in full kit, together with exercises such as push-ups and sit-ups. Invariably a liberal sprinkling of well-placed kicks and punches helped you along the way! We spent many a morning listening to the thunder of boots roar past our dorm as the day's 'failures' endured their torment.

Breakfast was next on the day's agenda. The food was garbage! Powdered egg and milk in the morning, followed by meat-substitute at lunch and dinner. I, like many others, survived on food parcels as well as the odd meal from home. I entered the Police College at about just over 100kg in January 1986 and left some 30kg lighter in late April!

After breakfast, the day was split up into lectures, marching drill, self-defence and everyone's favourite, musketry. The day would be rounded off with the mandatory *opfok* around 17h00 just in case you had forgotten your place. This consisted of about half an hour of continuous exercise with three or four NCOs (non-commissioned officers) – usually sergeants between 18 and 20 years old – hurling insults in your direction along with the ever-popular motivational kick or clout.

The evening meal was followed by a compulsory two-hour study period carried out in complete silence. A shower and 'lights-out' would then complete the average day, unless you were down for guard duty.

As the base was large and had been the target of an ANC RPG (rocket-propelled grenade) attack, guard duty was taken reasonably seriously and required significant person-power. Shifts usually lasted four hours but this was left to the discretion of the officer-on-duty as extra guard-duty was a popular means of punishment.

The short straw was the 02h00 to 06h00 shift as you would have barely fallen asleep before having to wake up, ensure you were meticulously dressed, and report for duty at the armoury to pick up your weapon. Basically, it meant 24 hours without sleep!

The instructors in the musketry facility were okay guys in general. This was probably due to their being somewhat older and therefore more mature than the other NCOs who were barely out of high school. I was very impressed with the level of weapons training.

The firearms used were the R1 (the key assault rifle in South Africa at the time, using 7.62 mm ammunition in a 20-round magazine); the Browning semi-automatic shotgun; the Beretta eight-shot pump-action shotgun; the nine millimetre Uzi sub-machine gun; the Walther nine millimetre pistol; and the standard SAP handgun, the 16-shot nine millimetre Beretta. Every cadet was obliged to develop the ability to assemble and disassemble all these weapons, blindfolded.

Live firing took place on the College firing range and was usually enjoyable – except for one occasion. Whilst taking part in the competency evaluation with the Beretta pistol, a young instructor, no more than 20 years of age, took up position adjacent to me. My first shot hit the bull and he commented 'mooi skoot' (nice shot). Good start, I thought to myself. The following shot was not as accurate and instead of a comment this time I received a full-blooded smack across the back of my head! Concentrate (or words to that effect) screamed the instructor as he mouthed off insults relating to my English heritage.

I received a further two smacks during the testing, which I took as quite an achievement, given the pressure. You do try to concentrate when you are expecting a clout at any moment! There was no thought given to instruction. The attitude was 'just intimidate the hell out of them and they will shoot well!' This pretty much summed up the sadistic nature of some of the instructors in the force.

Teargas instruction was another interesting training exercise and, if nothing else, it fostered a healthy respect for the effectiveness of the weapon. In our case, a series of teargas grenades were set off in a gully on the shooting range. The platoon was then required to walk through the gas without protective masks! Running was not an option unless you particularly wanted punishment duty or a beating!

Teargas by name, tears by nature. After the exercise, the grass was littered with vomiting, rasping and crying cadets while the instructors looked on in amusement. Not a pleasant experience. I could not wait to get back to our dorm as my contact lenses had been impregnated with the teargas, making my eyes sting like hell.

Again, we were by no means the worst off. Other platoons, with more sadistic NCOs, were locked in their classroom with the teargas. The door was only opened when the instructors became tired of the entertainment. This was an experience too horrible to contemplate. But then that was the point of basic training – as anyone who has done it can testify.

It became clear at the College that apartheid was not restricted to race. In theory, instruction was supposed to be conducted equally in English and Afrikaans, but English was used only once a week on Wednesdays during morning parade. Over time it became so unfamiliar that even English-speaking cadets could not follow basic commands, leading to mass confusion when the camp commander issued the command 'by the left, quick march' to dismiss cadets from the parade ground. Often prayers and instructions that began in English would revert to Afrikaans after only a few sentences. No equality here.

In relation to instruction, racism was far less overt. Well, there weren't any 'non-whites' on the base so I suppose it was not required. At times, we were told that anyone who supported the ANC or non-racialism had no place in the SAP, and that support and love for the National Party and the country was basically one and the same. Sexist thinking was also fairly prevalent, and I remember one lesson where we were told that women could be considered to be provoking sexual assault by wearing skimpy clothing!

I learnt to keep my head down pretty quickly at Police College, particularly owing to my English heritage. The reality was that there was a fundamental distrust and enmity between Afrikaner and English-speakers. A fellow English-speaker in the platoon, Greg Shaw, failed to toe the line, resulting in severe consequences for himself and the platoon.

Greg was a fun guy and, as the only two Englishmen in the platoon, we became friends fairly quickly despite the obvious differences in our characters. Greg had a boisterous and outgoing personality which was not really suited to the strict Calvinist regime in place at the College.

Greg's first brush with authority got the entire platoon into conflict and probably laid the foundations for the treatment that was later meted out to him. He was refused leave by one of the instructors for a minor incident of insubordination. Some members of the platoon felt that he had been hard done by and went over the head of the NCO and appealed to a major, who was a lecturer in the academic unit, on his behalf. The major kindly rescinded the order and Greg departed on his weekend pass with the rest of us.

Not that easy I'm afraid. Upon reporting back for duty on the following Monday our NCOs informed us that our daily schedule had been altered and that we needed to learn to obey orders. We spent the entire day undergoing an intense *opfok*! We ran until we vomited, climbed ropes in the gym until our hands were raw and finally completed circuits of the mounted police unit in full kit, clambering up and over the stables, and landing in piles of horse excrement, until dusk! Point taken. None of us would be going over anyone's head again!

Of course, the girls in the platoon were excused from this punishment. One or two seemed to enjoy our pain a little too much for our liking, something for which we exacted our revenge a little later. During shotgun training we ensured that a particular girl was selected to demonstrate the correct manner of firing the weapon. The instructor asked her to hold the butt of the weapon away from her shoulder before pulling the trigger. Anyone who knows how to fire a shotgun will know that this is the wrong technique. Upon firing, the recoil sent the butt smashing into her shoulder, knocking her off her feet much to the amusement of those watching. Apparently, a lovely bruise came up during the following days. The girls seemed to get the message.

Our days were so long that everyone was desperate for any time off that could be obtained. Our platoon leader, in his wisdom, accepted an offer (order) from one of the NGK Church ministers for the squad to have an informal discussion with him around 22h00 one evening. Now no-one was thrilled as this would make us really late, but we all agreed to attend.

However, Greg failed to appear and when he could not come up with a reasonable excuse our platoon leaders were less than happy. They decided to teach him a lesson. Greg was placed on permanent guard duty for the remainder of our training, around three weeks or so. This meant that when he was not attending classes he would be on duty and of course, he never got any sleep. I guess the plan was to force him to quit or be caught sleeping on duty.

Some members of the platoon felt that he was being harshly treated and we obviously helped out where we could. In addition, some of the academic members of staff, who were, on the whole, fairly well disposed towards the cadets, turned a blind eye to Greg sleeping in class. He did well to hang in there, and passed the Police College with us in late April 1987.

The end finally arrived and we received our postings. Almost everyone was happy with their allocations, with Greg and I particularly pleased to be going home to Durban. However, mine carried a sting in the tail. My educational qualifications had led me to be assigned to the Durban Security Branch, or SB, as it was commonly known. This was not how my plan was supposed to work.

Again, some would argue that I could have turned the posting down but they would not be living in the real world. I would have been better off resigning. You didn't turn down the SB. They were seen as the cream of the crop and secondment to the unit was regarded as a plum posting. Refusal would certainly have put paid to any chance of a return to Durban and I would have been more likely to have been packing my bags for Soweto or some other dangerous deployment.

# 2

# Policeman

I reported for duty at CR Swart Square, the SB headquarters in Durban, in April 1987. While I was aware of the SB's reputation, I did not know what to expect. It's fair to say that my main feeling was one of trepidation.

I suppose my initial duties would best be described as 'gopher' to a certain Major Louwrens, a rather unpleasant individual, who was the head of the Point Investigation Unit. The Point Unit was primarily located in a house in the docks area of Durban while Major Louwrens and I worked out of CR Swart Square.

Louwrens was responsible for monitoring black youth activity and unrest in the local Durban townships, particularly Chesterville, in addition to acting as police spokesman/liaison on civil litigation arising out of the numerous 'torture' allegations made against the SB. It was here that I first became familiar with the use of systematic torture within the police.

Torture was common. While accompanying Major Louwrens to the Point Unit, in what became my key role as chauffeur, it was not unusual to hear the screams of prisoners being interrogated. As the house in which the Unit was located was set away from the surrounding premises, and these were mostly industrial, their cries could not be heard by the general public. I'm sure this was a key factor in the selection of the location.

My initial reaction to the experience of torture was one of disgust. Such actions can never be justified. My dilemma was what to do about it. More importantly, what could I do about it? I ran through every scenario available but found my options limited.

Option one was to go to Major Louwrens. At Police College we were told that torture was unacceptable and should be reported to our immediate superior. Well, Major Louwrens was directly involved in the torture so I figured he knew. No-go there. Ironically, during the 1990s Louwrens was praised by the ANC for his 'moderate views' and 'positive approach'!

Option two was to go higher up the chain of command. No-go there either. Prior to visiting the Unit one week, I chauffeured Major Louwrens and Brigadier Steyn, the head of the Natal SB, where the topic under discussion was the torture at the Unit. They were particularly concerned about how to better conceal evidence of torture since a group of visiting state prosecutors had noticed one of the leather 'hoods' used in interrogation. After this, it was clear to me that complaining to the top brass was out. Furthermore, I could not betray my true feelings to my 'colleagues' as they appeared to enjoy their work.

I can remember going home with a heavy heart after my first visit to the Point Unit Field Office. The only other alternative was to go to the press. But what proof did I have? I would have been just another liberal who was making up stories. Allegations of police brutality and torture were widespread, but providing concrete proof was another matter entirely.

Torture took many forms, but the key instrument of torture at the Unit appeared to be a procedure known as 'tubing'. Either a leather hood or 'wet bag' was placed tightly over the head of the detainee so that they could not breathe and removed when the torturer felt it was appropriate.

Of course, aside from its sheer callousness, this technique was extremely dangerous. Anyone would panic under such treatment and be unable to hold their breath for as long as normal. For an asthmatic or someone with a weak heart such actions could be fatal.

Another 'popular' method of torture was electric shock to the genital area – for both men and women suspects. The electric shocks probably accounted for the majority of the screams I heard from the interrogation rooms. This was clearly extremely painful and I believe, if carried out correctly, left few visible signs of mistreatment.

It is worth noting that under the security legislation at that time, a suspect could be held for a period of six months without trial or access to legal counsel. Therefore, there was more than enough time for injuries to heal before the suspect was released, thereby reducing the validity of his or her claims of mistreatment.

Another form of torture was the notorious 'helicopter' technique. The detainees' hands would be fastened behind their backs and their ankles tied together. A pole would then be placed through the restraints and the victim would be lifted into the air with the pole resting on furniture, suspending him/her face-down, below the pole. The prisoner would then either be spun around or simply left to hang.

This was an extremely uncomfortable position which made it very difficult to breathe. Once again, such torture left few visible signs of mistreatment. Physical violence was used, but usually on low-level suspects who would be unlikely to go to the press or make a fuss about their injuries.

In the end, I did nothing directly about the torture. I decided to bide my time and as it happened, fate intervened, and I had the chance later to expose the government funding of Inkatha. Although never present at any torture, my inability to do something to expose it haunts me to this day. It was a key factor behind my later actions.

I joined the SB in late April and I took leave prior to my wedding in early June, so in reality, I was only there for May. But it was long enough, I can assure you! After getting married in June '87 I found myself transferred to a new section of the SB called 'White Organisations'.

'White Organisations' provided a stark contrast to my previous posting. My new boss was Lieutenant Piet Brandt who turned out to be one of the most genuine well-meaning policemen I met in the force. This was a very different unit from the others – no torture here! Immoral and illegal actions, definitely, but I figured I could see out my four years if I kept my head down.

It seemed that torture was reserved mostly for black activists – at least the physical stuff. There were forms of harassment which I suppose you could say amounted to something like psychological torture, but nothing as bad as experienced by many black activists.

The general area of responsibility in 'White Organisations' was the monitoring of 'subversive activity' amongst the white anti-apartheid movement in the greater Durban area, and the securing of highly placed sources within the various organisations (Black Sash, the End Conscription Campaign, Institute for Democratic Alternatives for South Africa, the university Student Representative Councils, etc). 'White Organisations' was one of many sub-divisions of the SB in Durban. It was a fairly small unit with the call sign Alpha. Initially all staff were white but towards the late 1980s coloureds and Indians were also seconded.

There were many other sections of the SB. 'Black Organisations' (call sign Bravo) covered a similar area of responsibility to ours but obviously focused on black organisations in the Durban region. Township activity was of particular importance to the apartheid state and so the Bravo section was considerably larger than the 'white organisations', with a significantly higher workload. It's worth noting that all the senior officers in 'Black Organisations' were white.

C Section, or C1 as they were often called, was considered by many to be the SB's elite. It all depends on what you aspire to I suppose. They were responsible for monitoring all armed ANC activity within the region, though in effect, their network spread countrywide and as far away as Swaziland. They often collaborated with the C sections from other provinces when circumstances warranted.

In addition to investigating all ANC attacks in the Durban area they 'ran' ANC fighters called 'Askaris' who had been 'persuaded' to change sides and spy on their former comrades. These 'Askaris' played a key role in providing valuable intelligence that the Branch used to counter attacks from the ANC.

For the period that I served in the SB, C section was led by Colonel Andy Taylor with Captain Hentie Botha as one of his key assistants. It is important to note that virtually all the Charlie Section personnel applied for indemnity from the Truth and Reconciliation Commission for murders they conducted whilst carrying out their 'duties'.

The D Section established and monitored counter-intelligence duties within the SB in addition to carrying out many of the STRATCOM (Strategic Communication) activities. These are best described as forming part of a coordinated programme of disinformation, covertly conducted by the SAP and various state intelligence agencies, aimed at disrupting anti-apartheid opposition. The E Section was responsible for monitoring coloured and Indian anti-apartheid opposition, yet, once again, was under the command of a white officer!

The administration of the SB was the responsibility of F Section. Their most important function was to serve as a register for all the sources (spies) working for the Security Branch in addition to serving as the conduit for their payments. The section was ably run by Captain Mouton from his office on the 12th floor. Many of the top secret files, which I later stole, were stored in his office adjacent to the filing room.

G Section was tasked with monitoring the activities of the Trade Union movement, with a particular focus on the Congress of South African Trade Unions (COSATU), while H Section's area of attention was the United Democratic Front and Black Consciousness organisations such as AZAPO. There was also the Post Interception and Telephone Tapping Unit under the leadership of Lt Van Dyk, and a small 'Churches unit' together with satellite SB offices at the towns of Port Shepstone, Scottburgh and Stanger.

With a couple of exceptions then, the Security Branch was organised along racial lines. Further, almost all the officers in charge were white, even in the sections that dealt exclusively with black, Indian or coloured activists.

The SB was also racist in its practice. Blacks were able to rise up through the ranks and receive the same remuneration as whites, but they could not exercise the authority accorded to that rank unless they were working with other black staff.

The following example highlights this mind-set. There was a black Major Khumalo who worked on my floor whom I greeted on most mornings. I was a sergeant at the time and therefore four ranks below him. One day in the lift, when he replied with his usual 'Good morning, Sir' to my 'Good morning, Major', I said, 'Major, you outrank me. I say "Good morning, Major" and you say "Good morning, Sergeant"'. 'Yes, Sir', he replied. 'No Major, I call you sir as you are my superior', I said. 'Yes, Sir', he replied resolutely!

I suppose it was so ingrained that whites were to be treated as superior to blacks that nothing I said was going to make any difference. It goes without saying that we had separate toilets, eating areas and office facilities for blacks and whites.

I think I was assigned to 'White Organisations' because of my university connection, and monitoring the activities on campus was one of the prime functions of our unit. My partner was a young Afrikaner named Albert Swart, and we shared an office. Our first task was to find some sources, what civilians would call spies, to provide a flow of information. Sure, not exactly anti-apartheid work but infinitely better than my first experience of the SB.

My progression through the ranks was set because I had a degree. After two years of probation in each rank, I would automatically be promoted as long as I had been a good boy. Early days in 'White Organisations' went fairly smoothly since Albert and I got on well, and Piet was a pretty easy-going boss.

The surveillance of anti-apartheid activists was pretty effective, although lots of work. The Post Interception and Telephone Tapping Unit was one of the most important sections in the SB. This unit consisted of retired officers who were re-enlisted to carry out the somewhat tedious task of monitoring the postal and telephonic activities of selected anti-apartheid activists and organisations. Each day, a tape recording of conversations was made available for listening or transcription. This was obviously time-consuming, hence the need for retired officers.

Phone lines were tapped with the co-operation of the Post Office who linked us via the exchange automatically so that we could 'hook' any phone in the Natal region. Legitimate phone taps were obtained via a written motivation to the Postmaster General; however, many were routinely carried out without authorisation. In fact, it was not unknown for husbands to 'tap' the lines of their wives if they believed they were having an affair, or a rival business, if a commercial advantage could be obtained. (Many black officers went into the taxi-cab business in the late 80s.)

Virtually all postal items sent to the various anti-apartheid movements were intercepted, with funding being a particular area of interest. Cheques were frequently stolen and the proceeds used for the SB. There were also individual acts of personal theft. These cheques were paid into bank accounts of front companies or individuals that had been opened using fake documentation, often with the assistance of SB sources within the banking community.

Such misappropriation of funding had the spin-off of creating dissension and in-fighting within the ranks of anti-apartheid organisations who often accused individuals of theft or corruption, when in fact the SB was the real culprit. It should be remembered that all these activities were being mirrored in the various SBs around the country.

Concerning the spies, there were primarily three categories, or what we called 'sources'. The lowest level of informant was given a PN(G) number (Port Natal General), for example PN(G) 147. This source would be paid on a casual basis rather than by a monthly salary.

Generally, a source would have a principal handler and a co-handler as backup since policemen fall sick, are transferred, etc. Without alternative access, valuable information might have been lost. In reality, most agents jealously guarded access to their informants whenever possible, frequently flouting the co-handler doctrine.

All sources were required to sign both a registration form upon agreeing to work for the Branch and a receipt whenever cash changed hands. Each month a source payment form would be submitted to the commanding officer for signature in order to claim cash for the source. Here, you would list the number of reports that had been submitted, based on information provided by your source, together with an estimate of the funding such information warranted and the sums paid to the individual for the previous three months.

Usually, for a PN(G) source, this would be in the region of R200. Productive sources could easily earn anything from R500 to R2000 a month. Tax free of course! All out-of-pocket expenses whilst on operational duty would obviously be reimbursed. And you thought the government wasted your taxes...

Of course, once a source had signed up it was difficult if not impossible for them to discontinue working as an informer as the SB could always 'leak' their actions to either the press or their organisation. If the situation suited both parties, it was not uncommon for pseudonyms to be used in order to protect the source's true identity.

This practice led to a number of cases of fraud when policemen invented fictitious sources, getting friends/associates/relatives to sign the relevant documentation while using Branch hearsay and newspaper articles as the basis of their 'intelligence'. The state was defrauded of significant sums of money in this manner since there was little, if any, scrutiny of the actions of the handlers.

In the second category, informants were given a PN registration number. They would generally be better-placed sources who could expect to receive superior remuneration and possibly a monthly retainer, depending on their status.

In the third category, informants were RS (Republic Security Intelligence Programme) sources who represented the highest level of informant, with the possible exception of the Askaris. These sources were actually full-time police force members who received all the benefits accorded to a uniformed officer whilst they were on the payroll. If their cover was blown or they could no longer serve any useful purpose they would take up their position within the SAP, usually in the SB.

Many of the RS agents worked in the various university Students' Representative Councils around the country, because the police offered the considerable inducement of not having to complete two years' military conscription, together with the good old South African taxpayer footing the bill for their studies!

The profile of a typical source varied depending on the organisation the agent was attempting to infiltrate. Agents cultivated sources whenever the opportunity arose because they would invariably come in useful in some future operations. These sources may well have remained unregistered but could always be remunerated from 'Branch funds'.

In this way a contact working in the tax office might be useful in obtaining confidential personal financial information relating to a subject that we would not have had access to via official channels. I know that many of the false passports held by the members of C1 were procured in a similar way.

The selection of RS agents was generally done quite professionally, but of course there were exceptions, with none more spectacular than that of Brian Boucher. Here was an individual whose entire persona screamed 'police spy' yet he apparently managed to infiltrate the SRCs of both Wits and the University of Natal, Durban, with considerable success.

Consider the facts. Brian Boucher's father was a policeman, and Brian resided in police accommodation adjacent to police headquarters at CR Swart Square. Without any prior history of political activism and a dress sense more suited to downtown Pretoria, this man's background should have aroused serious concern among his student colleagues.

I was of the opinion that he went into the RS programme to pay for his university education as the cost would probably have been beyond his father's police salary. No sane agent would have attempted to infiltrate a source with such a difficult background to hide. It simply did not warrant the time or the expenditure.

Boucher briefly appeared in our section after the completion of his 'duties' before taking up the position of Commander of Point Road Police Station, having earned the rank of Lieutenant whilst serving as an RS agent.

In my experience, the reliability of sources varied. The Special Branch tried to accommodate this by requiring handlers to rate the trustworthiness of both the source and the reliability of the information in their reports. This was always written in Afrikaans on the reports as follows:

## Comment: Gary Cullen

It would be true that these organisations (and the ANC) were heavily infiltrated. However, the threats were those who became trusted. Not included in this group was Brian Boucher.

On his first day of orientation week he was quick to join the Projects Committee (the political committee). I was the Projects Officer. Brian wanted to engage me in deep discussion along the lines of whether I thought Lenin and Mkhonto we Sizwe (the ANC's armed wing) were great! He appeared to think so…

Even better, we knew his family situation and that his authoritarian father virtually did not allow him to wear long pants, but did allow him to be involved with the communists at varsity!

At national level in NUSAS, Brian Boucher was the big joke, an obvious spy. He got elected to the SRC so he had a right to be there. The belief was that his purpose was to draw the heat to allow others to go by unnoticed.

In the End Conscription Campaign (ECC), where a number of the Christians had a very 'love thy brother' and 'don't condemn attitude', spies were not hunted out because, in many cases, one could not be sure. It was felt that unless it was proven, people should not be typecast as spies. Mark Symonds was one such case. I never trusted him at all, there was no evidence. He just fitted the spy type. At the end of the day we stuck to legal politics and in that way we did not have to worry about how many ECC members were working for Branch…

Lastly, may I express my admiration for what Brian [Morrow] did as the whistleblower and in doing so for the right reasons, rather than money and ego? I cannot resist, however, to say that his story fully vindicates the stand of those of us who refused to serve in the SADF and who understood service in the police to be no different.

| *Waardebepaling van bron*<br>Truthworthiness of source | *Betroubaarheid van inligting*<br>Reliability of information |
|---|---|
| A. *Geheel en al betroubaar*<br>Entirely trustworthy | 1. *Bevestig deur ander onafhanklike en betroubare bronne*<br>Confirmed by other independent and trustworthy sources |
| B. *Gewoonlik betroubaar*<br>Usually trustworthy | 2. *Gewoonlik juis*<br>Usually reliable |
| C. *Redelik betroubaar*<br>Reasonably trustworthy | 3. *Moontlik juis*<br>Possibly reliable |
| D. *Nie betroubaar*<br>Not trustworthy | 4. *Waarskynlik juis*<br>Apparently reliable |
| E. *Kan nie beoordeel word nie*<br>Cannot assess | 5. *Kan nie beoordeel word nie*<br>Cannot assess |

The SB seemed to go about recruiting sources with remarkable ease. Money seemed to be a big incentive for many people. I remember being extremely disillusioned at how willingly individuals would agree to sell out their colleagues and beliefs in exchange for money and the like.

I had resolved from the outset to keep as low a profile as possible whilst remaining on the lookout for an opportunity to do something. Hence, my first priority was to recruit a few sources to ensure a reasonable flow of information so as to keep my superiors content. This was relatively easy under the command of Lieutenant Brand and Captain Moon, both of whom were less than zealous in their support of the system and made do with relatively low-level intelligence. Great news for me!

However, there was a period when the Unit was led by Captain Kruger, an extremely unsavoury individual, who demanded results and was not too concerned about the means used to obtain them. I think he also sensed that I was not the most motivated member of the SB.

Through personal contacts, and those of acquaintances, I managed to secure the services of several PN(G) sources at the University of Natal who provided useful general information with regards to events on campus, as well as two reasonably well-placed unregistered informants in the university administration.

In addition many of the younger operatives, in particular Albert and I, were provided with fake student IDs that allowed us to move around campus with relative ease, with the additional bonus of the use of all university sports facilities! These were the real deal provided by Steve Pelzer, Head of Campus Security, who had a good 'working relationship' with the SB. I don't think the university administration was aware of this relationship; I'm fairly sure this was a covert operation.

Back to my sources. It was common procedure to have as many aliases as possible and we regularly produced phoney Police IDs complete with a pseudonym and senior rank. These were useful if you had reason to use the operational resources of another station. People tended to respond better to instructions from a lieutenant or a captain.

For me however, the real coup came in the form of a PN source who simply wandered in off the street claiming to have information of use to the SB, and I was assigned to conduct the interview. I was somewhat taken aback to find that the individual was none other than a senior University of Natal academic, Dr Charles Ballard, whom I knew well from my time at UND. He was an American national who lectured in the History Department. In fact, I had attended his lectures and tutorials for the previous three years.

I have to say he was somewhat taken aback when I walked into the room where he was sitting! Whilst appalled at his actions, I soon realised that this was an opportunity too good to miss. I immediately asked him if he would consider working for the SB, to which he readily agreed. I gave him the code name of 'Ron'.

I think Charles Ballard's (PN5377) motivation to become a source for the Security Police was a mixture of political belief and greed. I think he felt that he deserved a better standard of living than his academic position allowed.

He certainly derived considerable financial benefit for his actions over the years, much of it visible in the numerous alterations he made to his house in Roseglen, especially the swimming pool and outdoor entertaining area.

We often met at his residence if he could not make it to one of our safe houses (locations where sources could be debriefed without the obvious risk of entering a police station). I felt that the safe houses were better suited from a security perspective but he didn't appear to be overly concerned. I didn't push it as he was the one taking the risk… It didn't matter to me either way.

His usual monthly retainer was never less than R500 but often topped the R1 000 mark if he was particularly active. One must bear in mind that this was tax free and that the state reimbursed him for all 'expenses' incurred whilst on operational duty.

In the grand scheme of things Ballard was a decent source, but not a great one. He never reached a position of real consequence in the university, or outside of it, but for me he was a Godsend! I now had a source that was privy to the views of the leadership of the University of Natal through his membership of the Joint Academic Staff Association.

Initially, he provided information relating to staff and administration activities on the UND Campus but, over time, expanded his intelligence-gathering to include the ANC and SACP (South African Communist Party) activities. Again, I must stress that this was not earth-shattering stuff but it afforded me a sound pool of intelligence that helped create the illusion that I was actually gainfully employed.

Charles Ballard: University of Natal Historian and Security Branch source. Picture from the flyleaf of Ballard, *The House of Shaka* (1998).

My pocket-book from that time, covering the period May 1990 to January 1991, indicates that he attended a number of ANC meetings in the Durban area as well as a SACP conference held in Johannesburg on the 29th July. Of course the SB would have met all his expenses including hotel, airline and incidentals, in addition to paying a healthy bonus for his hard work.

Ballard also monitored a number of meetings of the Institute for Democratic Alternatives for South Africa (IDASA) in the Natal area during this time, though I was always of the opinion that they were a front for one of the various South African intelligence agencies.

Ballard possessed the credentials to attend any anti-apartheid meetings, together with the charisma and intelligence to obtain information from unsuspecting activists. Lieutenant Brand took a liking to Ballard and insisted on being his co-handler, something that proved useful to me after my homecoming from the UK in July 1989. Brand was nice enough to 'return' Ballard to me, which at least gave me one source of reasonable information.

My other sources included a useful one in the University of Natal Black Students Society (BSS) and the South African National Students Congress (SANSCO), which my partner Albert had secured. I served as co-handler for source PN1807 until 1988 when Albert was transferred to the Murder and Robbery Branch, leaving me as the primary handler.

PN1807's motivation was money, pure and simple. Again, running an African source created a minefield of emotions but I consoled myself with the knowledge that the information was fairly low-grade and that at least he was getting the necessary finance for his education. He initially provided information on SANSCO activities on the UND campus, but later monitored their activities on the University of Durban-Westville Campus after he changed courses.

In an effort to protect his identity I de-registered him as a source prior to my six months unpaid leave in the United Kingdom and then re-registered him upon my return. While he was not in Ballard's league when it came to remuneration, he received a substantial sum of money over the years, given his personal circumstances.

In all honesty, the overwhelming majority of valuable intelligence from our unit of White Organisations came from just two individuals, Jenny Chapman and Keith Marallich. Now, here were two people who enjoyed their work.

I could never really work out Jenny's motivation as she was a young, intelligent English-speaker who displayed no outward appearance of racism or support for the regime. I think, for her, it was the 'game' rather than the ideology. She liked being the covert operative, manipulating events and history from the shadows. The unmarked cars, expense accounts and travel all appealed to her personality.

Keith, whilst also intelligent, had strong connections with the SB: his brother worked in 'black organisations' and his father in the Post and Telephone Intercept Unit, in addition to being an Afrikaner.

Working closely as a team of co-handlers, Jenny and Keith ran at least 15 high-ranking sources in local 'white organisations' ranging from the End Conscription Campaign and the Black Sash to the various SRCs at the Universities of Natal and Durban-Westville. Amongst these monthly retainer sources, were the full-time SAP members RS462 and RS447.

There was really very little at the SRC and the ECC that SB was not aware of. Jenny and Keith both ensured that their informants were arrested and at times were also the subject of harassment, in order to enhance their cover and reputation amongst their fellow activists. Each year, Jenny and Keith would travel to other regions in the country, most notably the Eastern Cape and Western Province, to vet potential RS and possibly PN sources for deployment in our area.

The logic was understandable. Outsiders would either stay in residence or in digs and would be able to devote all their attention to infiltrating their assigned organisations either on- or off-campus. In addition, their actions would not fall under the scrutiny of either close friends or family who might have found their recent political conversion unusual. They could start with a clean slate, so to speak.

All sources were provided with a background story (termed a 'legend' in intelligence-speak) if the situation warranted. White males had the obvious Achilles heel of having to complete military service and this often meant that sources joined the SB on completion of their primary degree. Obviously, locals who 'suddenly' became political and were in possession of an income without any visible means of procurement, either in the form of employment or parental support, were easily identifiable as potential Branch operatives.

Perhaps the main name I remember from my time in 'White Organisations' is Graham Jordan. He has to be one of the most despicable individuals I have ever had the misfortune to know, although one would have to concede there was a lot of competition for this title at the SB! I soon determined to have as little to do with him as possible, because of the obvious enjoyment he derived from his position. Further, unlike Jenny and Keith, Graham exploited his situation to further his own financial ends and he clearly derived pleasure from inflicting pain on others.

Graham had few sources, yet despite having a stammer, he displayed the most persuasive manner on the telephone I have ever witnessed. His ability to change persona and accent had to be seen to be believed. He made much capital out of one excellent PN source well connected to the UND SRC and, more importantly, the End Conscription Campaign, Mark Symonds.

Graham, however, had other talents that the SB considered useful. He was the frontman responsible for the procurement of both safe houses and the setting up of so-called 'front companies' used to either disseminate STRATCOM information or as a means of recruiting sources under a 'false flag'. We had a number of safehouses available: 101 on the Esplanade, a flat in South Beach near the Addington Hospital and another in the Morningside suburb of Durban.

Of course, if your name was Graham Jordan, such locations were perfect for private business transactions and illicit deals. Such personal use of tax-payers' money was seen by the vast majority of the SB as an acceptable perk. I could never understand the mentality. Jordan was also responsible for much of what could only be termed 'criminal activities' undertaken by 'White Organisations'. Willing participants undertook harassment of white anti-apartheid activists to encourage them to discontinue their actions. Some, like myself, never participated in such actions and, to my knowledge, no-one was ever forced to take part.

Common procedures were the smashing of car and house windows with bricks, slitting car tyres, daubing paint on vehicles, placing sugar in petrol tanks, ruining the interiors of vehicles – most policemen were adept at gaining access to cars – and making threatening phone calls.

Once again, there was little I could do to expose their actions without drawing attention to myself and concrete corroborating evidence was nigh impossible to provide. These types of actions only fuelled my desire to expose police hypocrisy and corruption.

This also placed me under great emotional strain as I could not discuss these events with anyone, although my anti-apartheid stance in any family discussion became even more entrenched. I became increasingly infuriated at the inability or unwillingness of my family and friends to see through the garbage that was fed to them via the South African Broadcasting Corporation (SABC) and the press.

It seemed clear to me that neither Lieutenant Brand nor Captain Moon had any real affinity for such actions but, since these had been sanctioned by Brigadier Steyn, they had little choice but to allow Jordan to run amok. Those involved in such attacks tended to be Branch members who had few, if any, sources and such activities provided them with a sense of purpose and a means to remain in the unit.

In addition, their actions accorded them an enhanced status since most members of the Branch took great delight in the anguished complaints of the victims to the media, especially when the blame was apportioned to unidentified white right-wingers.

It's important to note that there was no real risk of Branch operatives getting caught vandalising property. Unmarked police cars with false number plates were used in all the attacks. There was a huge selection of false plates at CR Swart available for such 'operational duties'. Surveillance of the individuals concerned in conjunction with phone taps afforded the perpetrators the luxury of knowing all the movements of the victim(s), together with the information provided from the various sources.

Finally, if anything went wrong, the SB appeared to be extremely confident that any investigation by the uniformed branch of the SAP would be inconclusive. The code of silence was particularly effective in the police.

The low point of my time in 'White Organisations' must be the harassment of journalist Billy Paddock, on instructions from Brigadier Steyn, overseen by Captain Kruger and carried out with relish by Graham Jordan and his band of cronies. Paddock, a local left-wing journalist, had served a one-year jail term as a conscientious objector, having refused to be conscripted into the South African Military.

Conscientious objectors publicly refusing to serve in the Defence Force, Durban 1989. Security Branch source Mark Symonds partly concealed under the 'o' in 'to serve' on the banner. Laurence Piper standing directly behind Bishop Hurley's left shoulder.
Source: *Daily News*

He had had the temerity to write articles attacking the methods and tactics of the SB and it was decided that he should be 'taught a lesson'. The logic was that if he was 'persuaded' to spend more time on his personal problems he would not be in a position to devote as much attention to his professional duties.

Aside from the obvious moral objections, one has yet again to question the logic of this strategy: the Branch was to assign valuable resources to force Paddock to relocate to another area where one would expect he would simply resume his activities. And the point was?

Once again, I was not directly involved but kept an ear to the ground. The basic facts were that Graham Jordan and his merry band made life as unpleasant as possible for Billy Paddock and his family. Both his home and work telephones were tapped and his post intercepted. He could not move without police scrutiny.

Secure in their knowledge of the family's movements, Jordan and his team employed the usual Branch's niggly tactics of harassment, but it was the sheer pleasure they, particularly Jordan, derived from their 'work' that had to be seen to be believed.

Jordan would arrange to have the electricity of the Paddocks cut when he knew they would be away for some time. He arranged for the delivery of various items to the Paddocks' home that they had obviously not ordered, such as large quantities of sand, building materials and electrical items, and then took great delight in listening to Billy's phone conversations with suppliers when he took them to task. Phoney ordering was not a difficult task as Jordan had all of Billy's bank account numbers and electricity accounts readily at hand.

There was no level to which he would not sink. Branch operatives broke the Paddocks' windows with airgun pellets and damaged their car. Flowers were delivered to Billy's wife, Carolyn McGibbon, to sow dissent in their marriage, but the most despicable act was to send a Funeral Home hearse to their house at the dead of night as the parlour had been informed that their child had died.

Now as fate would have it, Billy Paddock, of whom I had frankly never heard prior to working in the SB, needed to visit CR Swart to see Major Louwrens in order to retrieve some personal items that had been confiscated in a Branch raid. For some reason, I was assigned to sit in the meeting and for a brief moment, while we were alone in the room, we struck up a conversation – probably to fill the rather awkward silence!

It has to be remembered that, while I was known to be somewhat of a liberal, by Branch standards – admittedly an easy task – I could not simply express my sympathies and knowledge to every person that I met, particularly given the number of sources SB evidently had at their disposal. I mentioned to him (quite stupidly and naively) that the answer to his harassment might have its origins in the force but sadly I lacked the courage to expand on this before Major Louwrens entered the room.

Thankfully, Billy did not mention my name when he went public with his plight. Typically, the police denied all culpability and blamed 'white right-wing extremists'. Well, it was half-true, right-wing extremists all right, but working for the SAP! With increasing levels of publicity being assigned to the case, Jordan was given direct orders from Brigadier Steyn to close down the operation.

**Comment: Carolyn McGibbon**

A few details differ, but other than that Brian Morrow's account is very accurate. In fact, until Brian's revelations, I did not know who had done this. The force that terrorised our happy little home for more than a year was a nameless, faceless monster. We knew that agents of the state were at work, but we did not know who they were. We tried to joke about it. Billy used to say: Paranoia is thinking you have four security policemen following you, when in fact there are only three.

It is hugely gratifying to read what Brian says. I have spent the better part of my life, twenty years as a journalist, uncovering the truth about other people's lives.

To be given the truth about my life, without asking, is like a huge present. A real gift. Thank you. It is the best present you could have given, Brian. I am so thankful.

Billy was doing his job as a news photographer at a time when the world was watching South Africa. He felt a deep personal need to expose what was happening in the country. He had 'contacts' within the banned ANC and often his pager would go off in the middle of the night, alerting him to the latest guerrilla attack. As far as I can remember, the campaign of harassment began after one of these incidents.

On one occasion, Billy received a message that a bomb had gone off at a spot quite close to our home in McDonald Road in Glenwood. He jumped out of bed and was at the scene in minutes. Then a second bomb exploded. The photograph he shot at the scene was beamed around the world. It showed the vivid horror of a man alight running from the bomb scene.

But Billy was deeply troubled by his experiences. He said he could not get the smell of burning human flesh out of his nose. The smell was similar, he said, to the sickly sweet smell of roast pork. We ate mainly vegetarian food around this time.

Police were alerted to the work he was doing and he was subjected to numerous arrests. Over a one-year period he was arrested 10 times. Usually at a political event, he would be among the first to be arrested. Fortunately, his lawyer friends would get him out, but his frustration levels were at boiling point.

Billy made it his mission to rattle the military establishment, becoming the first Christian conscientious objector to oppose the Defence Force. Billy was sentenced to spend a year as a civilian prisoner in Pretoria Central Prison with murderers, rapists and other common criminals. The traumatic experience did not break him, but made him even more determined to fight the system. In the late 80s it was impossible to predict the birth of democracy around the corner. It felt like we were living inside a pressure cooker from which there was no escape.

While Billy was making his mark as a press photographer, I was juggling being a mother and working as a reporter at the *Sunday Tribune*. Our daughter, Ro, was a tiny little baby when we had our first police raid. She cried unceasingly. At first she slept in the section of the bedroom facing the road, but after the security police smashed the window next to her cot, and sent the funeral parlour 'to collect the body', we moved her to an inside room. I struggled to produce breast milk with the tension and she failed to thrive.

Billy adored her and called her 'Spiderball'. He took her for long drives to help her get to sleep. She was the highlight of our lives and despite the harassment, I remember saying that the time the three of us shared after her birth was the happiest time of my life.

I hold Graeme Jordan and his cronies partially responsible for the break-up of our marriage, as we felt the only way to avoid continued harassment was to leave Durban. We did this, and our instinct was rewarded. Apart from one incident, the harassment did not continue. However, Billy was unable to find a job in Cape Town. Unemployment hacked away at his self esteem and when the opportunity arose for him to find work in Namibia, which was on the verge of independence, Billy took it, saying that I should follow.

But the sudden wave of freedom that hit him outside of South Africa was intoxicating. Within a few weeks he sent me a letter, saying he had decided he needed his freedom and wanted to leave the marriage. I stayed in bed for two days, paralysed with shock, and then got on with my life.

I don't think Billy was ever the same after the harassment. Friends say that he went mad from the Security Branch antics and I think there is an element of truth in this. Billy Paddock was killed in a car accident, soon after the dawn of democracy in 1994. I have no reason to suspect that it was not an accident.

The tragedy, I believe, is that Billy could have made a huge difference in post-apartheid South Africa. He lived and breathed the need to make a difference in society. I have no doubt that, had he been alive today, he would be an editor of a significant publication.

He would be challenging us to question our values, our aspirations. I think he would make us sleep uneasily at night, knowing that there were many people who did not yet have homes, years down the line of our democracy. He would prickle our consciences about our rampant materialism for the latest cell phones, cars and expensive homes. He would make us think deeply about who would make the ideal president.

## Comment: Graham Jordan

I would say 80–85% of what Brian Morrow says is true. You must remember that I was doing my job in a situation where it was basically a war, and yes, there were some fun and games but nothing too bad. Despite it being a war I never killed anyone.

The one claim that is clearly not true is that we sent the hearse for Billy's child. It was meant for Billy. You must remember that intelligence agencies all over the world, well, the non-communist ones, had rules and regulations and I stuck to those. It would be going a bit far to send the hearse for the child.

The other thing to remember is that it wasn't just Branch involved with Billy Paddock. The military and NIS were also players – and Billy wasn't always that popular with his colleagues at Reuters – so maybe some of that stuff came from them too.

Brian Morrow wasn't that senior in Branch, he didn't know very much outside of a very specific situation. As a professional policeman I was loyal to the previous government and did my job, the senior people knew what was going on, just as I am loyal to the new government.

Two other memories from this time stand out. The first was the funeral of two ANC 'terrorists' who had been killed in the infamous Piet Retief mini-bus massacre in the Northern Transvaal. As fate would have it, I was 'lucky' enough to be on call during the funeral of Lenny Naidoo, one of the victims of the massacre.

The funeral was only permitted under strict criteria based on the State of Emergency legislation in operation at that time and took place under heavy police surveillance.

Whilst on duty during the day in the Durban suburb of Chatsworth, I struck up conversations with a number of local residents and mourners who commented that it was unusual to meet a policeman who was responsive to the needs of the community. I had simply been polite and respectful at a funeral, a simple human act of decency that I would expect of anyone.

Well, as the funeral progressed, it became clear that the organisers would not be able to finish by 16h00, a clear stipulation of the emergency regulations. One of the members of the family approached me and asked if it would be possible to arrange an extension to the scheduled time, given the number of mourners.

I agreed to take their request to the SB Commander in charge of the operation, but he simply refused point blank. I was bluntly informed in Afrikaans that the order was for 16h00, and 16h00 is what it would be. As a sergeant I was outranked and in no position to countermand his order.

Now it must be remembered that this had been a peaceful funeral, taking place in a built-up residential area with numerous locals, among them children, who had little, if any, association with the deceased. Here was an opportunity to build bridges with the community and portray a positive image of the SAP. Not a chance! I sadly conveyed the news to the family who said they would do what they could to finish on time.

As 16h00 approached the commander used his loud hailer to inform all present that they would be participating in an illegal assembly under security legislation and that they should disperse immediately. At exactly 16h00 he gave the order to open fire with teargas and rubber bullets that were shot indiscriminately into the crowd and the surrounding houses. Uniformed police and soldiers used *sjamboks* (whips), thrashing anyone in reach.

Again, nothing remarkable, but I simply could not believe what I was seeing. This was simply not right! A peaceful event had been turned into a nightmare, not by the left-wing radicals as the SABC so regularly informed us, but by the bloody police, the people meant to protect society! That this could have been so easily averted only added to my sense of injustice.

Unfortunately, I had to endure a repeat performance in KwaMashu at the second funeral, with similar consequences. Here, a far more militant crowd engaged the police in running battles with stones, but the heavy-handed response (indiscriminate shotgun fire/teargas/and rubber bullets) once more affronted me, especially as the conflict was precipitated by the SAP and not the local mourners.

There appeared to be a total lack of empathy on the part of the military because the individuals concerned were 'terrorists' and therefore the feelings and sensibilities of their families, friends and next-of-kin were not worthy of consideration. A group of mourners who bravely attempted to place an ANC flag over the coffin (what actual difference would it have made?) were viciously assaulted and dragged away to waiting police vans.

I was not a happy bunny after both incidents, I can tell you, particularly when watching the SABC coverage of both 'riots'. Their version bore very little resemblance to the actual events, once again placing the blame squarely on ANC agitators. And of course, the watching white public took all this on board as fact ...

The second, and clearly criminal, act during my time at the Branch was the bombing of the Metro cinema in West Street, Durban. The rationale behind the bombing was to provide the Minister of Law and Order, Adriaan Vlok, with a reason to ban the screening of *Cry Freedom*, a film about the life and murder of Black Consciousness activist Steve Biko.

Having failed to have the film banned via legal means, Vlok ordered the SB to plant bombs in cinemas around the country so that the distribution could be halted on the grounds of public safety. Bomb experts from the C section carried out the attacks, and the film was withdrawn from South African cinemas; yet another case of gross abuse of state power on the part of both the government and the SAP while the white South African public carried on with their daily lives, blissfully – and contentedly – unaware of the covert actions carried out in their name!

And then my opportunity came. I discovered the Inkatha files.

# 3

# Thief

I did not set out to expose the relationship of the SB with Inkatha. I mean, every policeman knew that the both the South African Police and the government favoured Inkatha, but I had no idea that they were on the payroll.

Actually, my original plan was to uncover the identity of the key sources used by the 'White Organisations' section, but security was too tight. I had to make do with the documents I could obtain, which were the files of the lower level 'White Organisations'. These were all that I had official access to.

To begin with, I uncovered a range of stuff including the covert funding of the right-wing NSF (National Students Federation) by the SB. Basically, the documents showed that the NSF was a SB front. The plot was to counter the anti-apartheid 'propaganda' of the various university SRCs affiliated to the liberal National Union of South African Students (NUSAS).

For example, I found documents on Project Jackal and Operation Aristotle. Project Jackal was an attempt to forge connections between the NSF and the Inkatha Youth Brigade, and Project Aristotle was one of various humanitarian activities undertaken by the NSF in the violence-stricken Durban townships. The idea was to give the NSF a 'human face' and non-racial credentials to recruit 'do-gooders' from the local campus.

It was widely suspected that the NSF was a government front, but this documentation proved it. I also found names of the students that the SB recruited as 'full-time' agents, so to speak. Their mandate was to rise as far as possible within the structures of their local university SRCs.

I thought about going public or leaking these documents but decided against it. It was interesting stuff, but would hardly bring the government to its knees. I wanted something on a grander scale and the fact that the government was funding these organisations, meant that it was more than likely that they had fingers in other pies...

It crossed my mind that I would be a useful source for the ANC, but again, given the level to which the various apartheid intelligence agencies had penetrated the organisation I never felt comfortable enough to approach any activists with a view to working as a double agent. I just didn't know who to trust.

Other than Inkatha, the closest I got to a really big issue involved the SB dealings with Askaris. Over time it came to my attention, from office gossip and conversations, that there was a 'farm' operating down the South Coast where captured 'terrorists' were interrogated and housed if they agreed to become Askaris. If they refused they were killed and their remains buried on site.

I found this fascinating and it became a sideline quest to find the precise location of the mysterious 'farm'. As a 'White Organisations' operative my options were extremely limited since the SB operated very much on a 'need-to-know basis' and I was not privy to any C1 operational detail. However, people do talk...

An opportunity arose one day when C1 operative Laurie Wasserman needed backup for a covert meeting with three Askaris. The office must have been empty of other SB staff for him to ask me! Anyhow, I had to 'watch his back' while he debriefed and paid the informers. I was in no position to decline and, truth be told, was quite interested. Meeting turned 'terrorists' seemed to be an exciting opportunity and I thought to myself, 'Who knows, I might learn something?'

The meeting took place at one of the rear gates of Kings Park Stadium. It was surreal how the rest of the world carried on with their daily grind, blissfully unaware of the covert underworld in their midst. Anyhow, Laurie parked his car across one entrance away from the road and out of sight of prying eyes, thus providing some cover. I positioned myself behind the bonnet with my Uzi at the ready – the engine block would provide protection if we were attacked – doors stop bullets only in movies.

Askaris could never be trusted for a number of reasons. They had changed sides once, so they could do so again. Furthermore, they were armed. The SB provided Soviet Bloc weaponry such as Makarov, Tokarev and Stechkin machine pistols. These were dangerous men (and women) with very little humanity left in their souls.

The meeting took place without incident, but I remember being amazed at the cash that changed hands. Laurie handed over thousands of rands to each informer before they departed in separate directions. Lucrative business, I thought to myself.

Upon leaving, Laurie said that he had to swing past the 'farm' for something and would I mind if we did not go straight back to CR Swart. 'Brilliant!' I thought to myself, 'what an opportunity!' I told Laurie it was fine by me as I had nothing pressing to do back at Branch.

We set off down towards the North coast and were approaching the Blue Lagoon onramp for the freeway when he suddenly said that he would drop me off at the SB after all. His training and intuition must have kicked in, as the precise location of the farm was meant to be known only to C1 operatives. Even a highly regarded and trustworthy agent such as Wasserman would have been in trouble from his superiors if he had given away the location of such a secret to someone who was outside the unit.

Lawrence Gerald Wasserman (AM4508/96) made seven applications for amnesty to the Truth and Reconciliation Commission in 1999 and 2000.

He admitted to a wide range of illegal actions and human rights abuses including:

- the killing of 16 ANC/MK members and anti-apartheid activists; the illegal abduction of 10 ANC/MK members and anti-apartheid activists; including 2 from Swaziland, in the process breaking border regulations;
- the assault torture of 7 ANC/MK members and anti-apartheid activists;
- the unlawful arrest of 6 ANC/MK members and anti-apartheid activists;
- defeating the ends of justice in 4 cases;
- the unlawful possession of arms in 3 cases;
- the unlawful disposal of human remains in 2 cases;
- desecration of the bodies;
- failure to report death;
- housebreaking; and
- malicious damage to property.

He was granted amnesty on all counts bar the abduction, unlawful detention, killing, unlawful disposal of the body and defeating the ends of justice in the case of Ntombikayise Khubeka (AC/2001/124).

For full details of the findings, see the Amnesty Decision transcripts AC/2000/039, AC/2000/135, AC/2000/232, AC/2001/084, AC/2001/099, AC/2001/112, AC/2001/124 on the TRC website [http://www.doj.gov.za/trc/amntrans/index.htm].

The TRC testimony by Laurie and C Section operatives repeatedly referred to an abandoned SA Railways and Harbours shooting range at Winkelspruit, but this farm was in the Tongaat/Verulam area north of Durban. At the time, not finding the farm was a major let-down as I knew that the existence of Askaris would be major news, particularly if they could be linked to illegal activities. As it turned out, I was correct, but an opportunity never presented itself to obtain concrete evidence of their actions.

But then I found the Inkatha documents. In early 1988, during a quiet moment in the filing room, I decided to see what one of the cabinets near the 'White Organisation' files contained. I was amazed to discover that the SB was providing financial aid to both Inkatha and their trade union arm UWUSA. Indeed, based on the information outlined on one particular document, the government had virtually created UWUSA.

This relationship was confirmed by more documents that I discovered over the subsequent two years. In fact, obtaining documents that could categorically prove the existence of a link between the police (and therefore the government) and Inkatha became my prime motivation. By the end of my 'thieving' days I had over fifty in my possession.

When I found the first document I was both stunned and elated. I realised that now I had something that I could use to expose the duplicity of the government. The documentary evidence I could gather would make it very difficult, if not impossible, for them to talk their way out of it as they had done so many times in the past. I realised that this information had the potential to inflict serious harm on the government; definitely more so than unmasking the identity of a couple of spies or SB connections with the NSF or IDASA. This was probably as big as it could get.

How was it that I could just stumble across these secret documents? A mixture of good fortune, coupled with making the most of the opportunities that presented themselves. It is one thing to have them available, but quite another to actually remove them from both the filing department and the building. To understand this, it helps to know more about the layout of the building.

The Durban Security Branch was located between the 12th and 15th floors at the Police Headquarters at CR Swart Square. The SB could only be accessed by elevator from either the ground floor main lobby (this was the approach members of the public and uniformed SAP would use), or from a secure entrance next to the underground car park that required an access code. The lift was in a separate shaft to the others in the building and only went to the 12th floor.

Upon reaching this level you would step out into a foyer where a retired police officer behind a bulletproof perspex screen would either open a solid door electronically to allow you access (if he recognised you as a SB member), or make you wait in one of the two guest rooms until a Branch operative came down to meet you.

The stairway connection to the 11th floor had been secured with a solid metal gate similar to those used in the police cells. This was kept permanently locked and only the very senior officers had access. I never used the stairs, not even once in five years. On reflection, I don't think we would have passed current fire safety procedures!

The files I discovered were kept in the filing room on the 12th floor immediately to the left of the entrance. It may seem strange now in the era of computers, but this was the late 1980s and early 1990s and everything was kept on file in metal cabinets. The only photocopier was also located in this area. Very handy! There was also a shredder on each floor.

The really top secret stuff in the SB was housed in either Captain Mouton's office directly adjacent to the filing room or in Brigadier Steyn's office down the corridor. All source registration and covert operation data were stored in these locations and I had no realistic means of gaining access to these. However, there were cabinets containing 'lower level' evidence housed just at the entrance of the filing room. Captain Mouton's office was just not big enough. It gives you some idea of how much covert stuff was going on at the time. These were often left open while staff worked on them.

Basically, there was a level of trust of any other Security Branch members. That was the one overriding flaw that led to my ultimate success. The SB worked on the assumption that their vetting procedures would not allow anyone into the SB who did not share their views and who therefore did not support apartheid. Big mistake!

Still, I faced numerous challenges in my quest. Working in 'White Organisations' meant that, technically, I had nothing to do with Inkatha as it fell under the 'black section' sphere of influence. Therefore, I did not have access to Inkatha files as part of my direct employment, until some time later when I was 'demoted' to the filing room, but I figured I would keep my eyes open just in case.

Fate intervened too, none more so than when Captain Mouton's office was painted. Cabinets previously out of my reach were suddenly available in the filing room. I could not let this opportunity go to waste. A number of key documents, particularly the cheques revealing clandestine payments to Inkatha for rallies at Kings Park, were obtained during this period. An example of how often the little things you overlook cause the greatest problems!

In order to steal a document I would wait until nobody was looking. Then I would take a file and then move right away to the 'white area' cabinets and scan the contents as quickly as I could, on the lookout for incriminating information which I could photocopy. Each cabinet had numerous dossiers so no one would spot a missing folder unless that was the one they were looking for.

Photocopying was challenging in itself since I had to wait until the room was clear and hurriedly take my chances. On a positive note, the copier was tucked away in the corner, out of sight of almost all in the room. These were extremely tense occasions because being caught with the documents would have made it difficult enough for me to talk my way out, but being found making copies would have made it downright impossible.

After hiding the papers in my shoes, I would leave the building early in the morning, often directly after the 07h30 morning conference, as this was a busy period of the day when staff were coming and going, thus offering me some cover. I would head home and bury the documents in a box in my garden.

If the SB had caught me, I have absolutely no doubt in my mind that they would have killed me. The only debate would have been as to the means and how long I would have been tortured before being executed. I would have been viewed more contemptuously than the outspoken white liberals or black activists since I was 'betraying' both the force and my race.

As it was, I experienced a number of close calls. You have to realise that this was a very long process carried out over two years. The first crisis occurred thanks to my long-running battle with technology. My lack of skill and luck with mechanical equipment is legendary. One day whilst copying a particularly good document the bloody photocopier jammed. I did the obvious and panicked. What the hell was I to do?

I returned the original to its file and fled to my office, maintaining a composed and calm exterior to other SB members that I encountered. Once I cleared my thoughts (and changed underwear!) I knew I had to go down and retrieve the jammed document. Obviously, it contained no incriminating evidence in itself, but if found they would know someone was copying highly sensitive material.

This is one of the numerous occasions where luck was on my side because when I returned, the copier was still jammed and no-one else was waiting to use it. I forced open the machine, almost certainly breaking it, retrieved the document and immediately shredded it. I should have kept it and added it to my collection but I really wasn't thinking straight.

Copy of cheque to Inkatha for R100 000 of 11 November 1989.

This whole incident scared the hell out of me and I decided that there would be no more photocopying, and I embarked on an even more audacious plan: to take original documents from the file. Crazy I know, but it made sense to me.

Taking originals reduced my chances of being caught even though it may have alerted the SB that documents were being taken. I did this because it took less time to take the originals than make a copy; plus, the way the files worked was such that the first page of each file contained an index of the documents in it. Of course if someone needed to use a document that I had removed, they would know that either they had a very bad insect infestation or someone was taking documents. However this was unlikely as the files were simply a means of storing information, much in the same way as photos are stored in albums. In reality, how often do you actually look at them?

For a while, I kept on taking the files. Then from January until June 1989, I took unpaid leave and my fiancée (Michelle) and I went to the UK for six months. The trip was something of a dress rehearsal to see if we could fit into the lifestyle of the UK. I suppose I saw the end of my four years of National Service as a potential departure date but stayed on until I felt I had obtained sufficient information and Michelle felt more at ease with our decision. I guess, in part, I was always going to leave the country. Anyhow, upon the resumption of my duties in July 1989, I did not exactly work myself to death as I was very close to serving out my time in the force. Ironically, it worked in my favour.

I had been required to transfer my sources to other handlers prior to my 'vacation' so I really was starting from scratch, other than for 'Ron'. In addition, my boss had been replaced by a racist, apartheid apparatchik named Major De Beer, and a certain Warrant Officer Keith Marallich, although fortunately their role assumed more of a supervisory nature with Captain Moon (a fairly nice guy, in the wrong place and time) taking charge later in the year.

Keith was one of the more intelligent officers, and had probably realised that I was not as enthusiastic about my work as I should have been. In addition, I believe he was aware that I had the potential to be a successful operative if I was motivated. I found it both amusing and comforting to know that they were completely unaware of my actions and that I was indeed working very hard in my own way – to expose their illegal and corrupt actions.

Anyhow, I was summoned to a meeting with De Beer and Marallich to answer for my lack of productivity. OJ Simpson's legal team would have been hard pressed to organise a defence and I was duly reprimanded. Ironically, my punishment was to serve half-days in the filing room until further notice! Isn't the world a funny place? Talk about an opportunity. I now enjoyed virtually unrestricted access to all documents coming into the SB and every reason to have them in my possession.

I received the news with the required glumness since this was seen as a demotion for a field agent. Real men didn't work in the filing room! In reality, I was elated. Many of the key documents relating to the provision of financial assistance to Inkatha after the release of Nelson Mandela were obtained in this period. I have never had the opportunity to thank both De Beer and Marallich for their actions. Thanks guys!

**Comment: Keith Marallich**

Brian's account is basically true as far as I can remember, although I never had the authority to 'demote' him to the filing room. My rank was never high enough for that. Perhaps De Beer had that authority, I can't recall. As I didn't work much with Brian I don't remember much about him, in fact if I saw him today I doubt I would recognise him.

It's impossible to know exactly how many documents I stole since often a single document might run to ten pages. The top secret document drafted by Major Louis Botha outlining why Buthelezi and Inkatha should receive covert funding, written on 13 February 1990, is a prime example. Sadly, I only had size nine feet. Certainly, I took more than 50 documents over the entire period, numbering from a single sheet to up to 10 pages. I was a busy man. Not too difficult as I wasn't doing much else!

But then, people started to notice something was up. Within a couple of months of my return in July 1989, the admin staff in the filing room (who numbered three, counting Captain Mouton) clicked. This came to my attention at a meeting convened by my boss at the time, Captain Moon. He informed the section that dossiers were being stolen and that if anyone present was involved it would be best for them to stop the practice immediately. I, of course, maintained a facade of bemused ignorance.

I don't think they were on to me personally, but they were certainly aware that someone was taking top secret classified information. As one of the few English-speaking members of the SB, I guess my name would have come under discussion along with other known 'liberal' members. English-speaking SB members were few and far between and were never really accorded the same status as Afrikaner operatives, with the possible exception of callous killers such as Laurie Wasserman who, when considering his self-admitted murderous track record, seemed to see killing as a badge of loyalty.

Around this time, a counter-intelligence unit was set up in the SB, probably in response to my actions, under the command of Lieutenant Viljoen. My first encounter with direct action, instituted by the counter-intelligence unit, came as a complete surprise and somewhat of a reality check as to the possible consequences of my actions.

It was the end of another day, about November 1989, and my mind was a million miles away as I stepped out of the crowded basement elevator of the SB car park. Suddenly harsh voices rasped out commands in the claustrophobic passage; men and women were herded into separate groups; all clothing and briefcases in our possession were thoroughly searched.

The knowledge of my covert theft of documents created a heightened state of fear on my behalf although I was not in any immediate danger. I was not naïve enough to leave the SB at the end of the day in possession of incriminating documents. Nevertheless, the brusque and aggressive manner in which the search was conducted by my 'brother' officers left me in no doubt as to what treatment awaited me if I was ever caught.

The searches continued intermittently over the coming months but after the initial shock they were easier to cope with. I found them fairly predictable as they were carried out at the end of the day and did not present any real hindrance to my activities.

More ominous and dangerous to my well-being and blood pressure were the surprise lockdowns that took place. One day in mid-1990 at about 15h00 we were all ordered via intercom to return to our offices and informed that no-one would be allowed to leave the building until further notice!

Well, you can imagine the thoughts that ran through my head. Were they onto me? Had they found out? Had someone followed me? Would I have to fight? Did I have the courage to fight as I could not possibly win? Would I try and bluff it out? And of course, at the same time, I had to maintain a composed façade and not betray my inner turmoil to my partner, Brian Stuart. Talk about an Oscar-winning performance! Brian, of course, was speculating away and I had to maintain the banter whilst my mind was in a whirl of emotions. Not easy I can assure you!

Although Michelle was not aware of my actual actions as such, she did know that I was up to something. We arranged that if I made contact and mentioned the word 'holiday' she was to find help (legal assistance, parents, pray, etc.) if I did not either see her or establish contact within a short period of time.

I discounted the possibility that our office phones could be tapped owing to the number of phones involved and the manpower required to monitor the tapes – it was basically beyond the SB's capabilities. So I phoned home to tell her about the delay (a perfectly natural response), mentioned our code word in the conversation and waited and waited. After a few hours the all clear was given and I went home.

During this entire time I did not tell Michelle what I was up to. My reticence was due to a combination of factors, the most important being the issue of safety. If Michelle was unaware of the plan, then there was less likelihood of her being considered a suspect if my actions were uncovered, and there would be little risk of her suffering any repercussions from the SB.

In addition, this was a choice that I had consciously made and it seemed unfair to burden her with the consequences of my actions. Furthermore, initially Michelle did not share either my innate opposition to apartheid or my interest in politics. In many ways she was a stereotypical example of the average white South African who had little or no experience of the injustices of apartheid and was not really overly keen to find out.

As regards the lockdown, I was not the target. They were looking for an agent who was conducting the fairly widespread practice of inventing 'ghost agents' for personal financial gain. Apparently, an agent was doing this in some style and his lavish lifestyle had come to the attention of senior management. I did not know his name because he worked in another section, but his actions sure scared the hell out of me!

They had another lockdown a while later and to this day I have never found out what that one was about. All these events were eroding my confidence, and two even more traumatic incidents triggered our decision to leave the country.

The first of these was a car accident. Actually, it was not so much the accident as the way that the SB handled it that disgusted me. It highlighted both the corrupt nature of the force and the code-of-silence ethos prevalent in the police.

Every six weeks or so, a squad of SB members were required to be 'on 24-hour call' ready to respond to any security-related incidents that might take place, from bomb blasts, surveillance duties and road blocks to raids. My misfortune was to be on call during the highly emotive period of 16 June, Soweto (Youth) Day, when the Soweto uprising of 1976 is commemorated. This was further compounded by being paired with Constable Njila and Sergeant Tinus Fick from the township unit, who had definitely seen one too many Rambo movies.

We were monitoring a meeting in the notorious C section of the KwaMashu Township in the north of Durban, home to many violent incidents against both police and locals, when we received a garbled message over our radios. Our radios were somewhat unreliable in the hilly townships and it was not uncommon to pick up only segments of a conversation. We received a call that indicated that some of our colleagues were under fire in the nearby vicinity. As it turned out, they had been under fire but had escaped unharmed, and were just passing on the information. Unfortunately, Tinus (and myself, I suppose) reacted as if they needed our assistance.

Now I would have handled the whole scenario very differently, but events went as follows. Tinus was driving and I was in the front passenger seat with Njila in the back. We all abided by the standard SAP practice of not wearing seat belts in case of a petrol bomb attack and were heavily armed with both Uzi submachine guns and R1 rifles. We set off at high speed with sirens wailing in our unmarked police vehicle, although our occupation was hardly a secret – two whites and a black wearing civilian clothes in a black township! Short of writing 'Security Branch' on the side of the vehicle you couldn't have made our true identity any more obvious!

I became increasingly nervous as Tinus was driving down narrow, untarred, potholed roads lined with residents commemorating Youth Day, at breakneck speed. The last time I glanced at the speedometer, Tinus was doing 160kph and we were approaching an intersection. I was genuinely terrified but along with Njila, maintained a macho silence. Instinctively, I slipped the seatbelt over my shoulder, an action that probably saved my life.

Suddenly, I saw a vehicle coming at a great speed on the road to our right and I shouted. Tinus swerved, but too late. The other car hit us, although in front of the wheel housing rather than on the driver's door. We were hurled sideways, rolling up an embankment before coming to rest upright in the middle of the road. I went headfirst into the rear-view mirror, slicing open my cheek, but the seatbelt ensured that I did not go through the front windscreen. Unfortunately, I received a blow from Njila's R1 rifle in the back of my head which knocked me unconscious.

Minutes later, I awoke to the sound of Njila's terrified cries as he struggled to escape the car which, by that time, had been surrounded by township youth shouting '*Bulala umlungu!*' (kill the white man). Njila would just have been an added bonus! He was certainly not in the running for the 'luckiest policeman of the week' award as he had already been the victim of two other petrol bomb attacks.

As I came round, some members of the crowd tried to attack me but my survival instinct and training must have kicked in and I pointed my 9mm Beretta pistol in the nearest face. They backed off. Njila had regained his R1 (which had bounced back from my obviously hard head) and managed to persuade the crowd that we were well placed to defend ourselves.

Still, the situation was tense as my Uzi submachine gun had been flung out the car in the collision. Would the crowd use it to open fire on us? Tinus had also been knocked unconscious in the crash, but he too now joined us, ensuring that the crowd did not attack while we radioed for assistance. Luckily, an army Buffel (armoured patrol vehicle capable of carrying a number of infantry) was nearby. They fired a couple of warning shots and some teargas which dispersed the crowd. We could now get medical assistance. The occupants of the other vehicle were also injured but sadly we could not provide any assistance owing to the circumstances in which we found ourselves.

We were surrounded by hundreds of irate township residents who, at the best of times, were not well-disposed to the police, never mind the SB. It was certainly one of the scariest moments of my life. By the time the situation was under control, the injured occupants from the other vehicle had been assisted by members of the crowd. At the time, we were all caught up in the emotion of the occasion and the first priority was to ensure our safety.

I had certainly come out of the crash with the greatest visible injuries out of the three of us, looking a bloody mess, but Tinus decided to act up almost immediately once our safety had been ensured. He mumbled to Njila and me, 'Who was driving the car?' testing the water with Njila to see if he would support an allegation that I had been driving. 'You were', Njila and I replied virtually simultaneously.

Basically, there was absolutely no chance of a black man driving if other white members were in the vehicle, unless a specific operation called for it. In the same way there was little chance that Njila rather than a white policeman would sit in the front. In addition, Njila was a colleague of Tinus from the township unit. Credit to him for not dropping me in a mess. Perhaps it reflects the different regard he had for Tinus and me.

Anyhow, back to Tinus. Sensing no success with this approach, he then proceeded to exaggerate his concussion in a desperate bid to buy time since he was fully aware that he would carry the can for the accident. Siren or no siren, he had driven straight through a stop sign and that was a clear contravention of our standing orders.

We were transferred to Addington Hospital for treatment. Well, Tinus and I were, but of course Njila being black... Tinus continued his academy-award performance pretending not to know his name, day of the week, month of the year… and was therefore kept in for observation, giving him more time to construct his story and arrange the appropriate audience.

I received stitches to the cuts on my cheek and skull but was informed that a CT scan was unnecessary. Only years later in the UK did I become aware of the full extent of my injury when, after being knocked unconscious in a football match, I was asked by the doctor: 'When did you sustain your fractured skull?' Another great legacy from the SAP!

After some time off I returned to the SB, to be informed that the circumstances of the crash were now somewhat different to my account. Tinus had indeed been busy! In the new version outlined to me by superior officers, most notably Major De Beer and Brigadier Steyn, we were the innocent party who had been viciously rammed by the occupants of the other vehicle who had failed to stop at the intersection. I know that I had received a bang on the head, but come on!

I was left in no doubt as to where my duty lay. I should support my brother officer and sign the statement that they had prepared. A copy of Njila's statement was shown to me corroborating the sanitised version, with the clear insinuation that, not only was I on my own if I stuck to my story, but if a '*kaffir*' could support Tinus, then so should I.

I reluctantly acceded to their 'request', secure in the knowledge that I would never be appearing in court to confirm my statement under oath. Actions of this type took a long time to bring to court and I knew I would be overseas soon. To an outsider, it would probably seem easy to take the moral high-ground and stick to your guns, but in reality, that was never an option. If I had refused to support their version I would have been ostracised, making my objective of obtaining documents all but impossible. I could also be certain of receiving the most dangerous postings, secure in the knowledge that no one would be watching my back in any contact situation.

All these events were eroding both my resolve and confidence and the final straw came in a fairly dramatic fashion. One evening, I went to collect the post and found an unmarked blank envelope. I opened it and read the following message with increasing trepidation:

> Having considered all the options, I am forced to approach you in this manner. My life is in very real danger and I need help desperately. I know of no-one else on the inside who is in a position to help me.
>
> I am desperate, otherwise I would not jeopardise your safety.
>
> If you agree to assist me, place the enclosed sticker on the back of your blue Golf and I will contact you again.
>
> Although I am a loyal supporter I must consider my own safety above that of others.

Well, it's difficult to actually put the emotions that I experienced at that moment into words but 'scared shitless' would suffice. I discounted the possibility that it actually came from an ANC member, as the contents were designed to imply. It was obviously from counter-intelligence at the SB, who clearly considered that I could be the leak at CR Swart.

Was it a wild guess? Was it based on my being an English '*rooinek*'? Was I under surveillance? Did I run or face my accusers? Michelle and I discussed the contents and I decided the only option was to brazen it out. If I was under observation then a sudden flight to the airport would have only confirmed their suspicions.

We decided to spend the night at her parents' home, a fairly feeble attempt to throw them off the scent and somewhat cowardly in dragging my in-laws into the situation, but we figured there might be some safety in numbers. My Uzi and Beretta were never far from my reach and any sleep was fitful as my mind raced with thoughts as to what might face me the following day.

I entered the SB in the morning, in turmoil. My instincts were shouting 'run' but I knew that the only realistic option was to stay and face the music. I immediately located Captain Moon and showed him the letter. The look on his face indicated that he clearly was not party to the scheme – he looked more frightened than me! I played the affronted, indignant 'you can trust me, I'm no traitor' role as if my life depended upon it, and it probably did.

Captain Moon passed on the message up the chain of command and I was left to sweat out the rest of the day. But now the decision had been made! It was time to leave the country – things were getting too close for comfort.

I heard nothing more about the mysterious message and presume that I was just one of a number of people who were being assessed as potential sources of the leak. I suppose the fact that I reported the 'contact' proved that I was trustworthy. The lack of follow-up itself indicated the true origins of the note: if the SB had considered it an honest attempt from an ANC operative to make contact, they would certainly have asked me to play along to uncover the person's identity.

Around this time, President De Klerk had been touring the US and Europe, being fêted by Prime Minister Thatcher and President Bush, banging on about the tragedy of the 'black-on-black' violence and how the police were simply impartial onlookers at this orgy of African tribal conflict. Any accusations of police collusion were derided and accusers were asked for evidence to support their allegations. Talk shows on Radio 702 with John Robbie were full of it and my blood boiled as I thought of the documents buried in the garden. Proof?! I'll give you bloody proof in spades…

# 4

# Whistleblower

When deciding to flee the country in 1990, I chose England because of the family connection. As I've said previously, my father was born in Durham and ever since I was a child, there had been a strong link with the UK, reinforced over the years by regular visits there. I never considered going anywhere else.

Since my intention was to expose the government, I didn't want to attract any attention when leaving, so I did things by the book. It would be exciting to portray my flight from South Africa to the UK as the heroic escape of some Donald Woods type, but the reality was rather more mundane. I simply tendered my resignation to the police, having served out my time. Then, under the pretext of going into business with my parents, Michelle and I departed for England in the grand comfort of the *Canberra* ocean liner. It had been rerouted via the Cape because the Suez Canal was inoperative due to the impending Gulf War.

I abided by standard police resignation protocols in order to avoid raising suspicion that I might be the SB mole. Any variation from the norm might have been interpreted as worthy of investigation.

We went by ship, partly because I'm afraid of flying! In addition, I felt that the customs inspection at the Port of Durban would be less rigorous than at the airports, given the novelty of liners in South Africa at the time. I also hoped that the sheer number of passengers boarding the vessel would mean that inspection by customs officials would be cursory at best. I was right. We came through customs unscathed with a veritable library of documents, the most sensitive stored in my boots, with the rest secured in the soles of my shoes in the luggage.

It was a really emotional moment when the *Canberra* left Durban harbour. Sure, I was relieved. We had made it out of the country with the evidence. But my relief was tinged with sadness. Deep down I knew that life wouldn't ever be quite the same again, and that I might not return home for some time.

It was pretty much plain sailing all the way to England, although our arrival in Southampton was extremely stressful. We were pulled over by a very overbearing customs officer clearly intent on searching our baggage. The weight allowance for sea travel bears no relation to the miserly 20kg allowed on planes. We had a heck of a lot of cases. The problem lay in the fact that hidden away in one of the bags were two cans of teargas that I had 'borrowed' from the SAP!

Old habits die hard I guess. Also, I always believe in planning ahead. It wasn't a teargas grenade but rather two cans of 'spray on' gas that the police routinely carried in a somewhat oversized aerosol can. They were black with a white dispenser. I had developed a healthy respect for the effects of teargas over the years and figured it was an effective non-lethal defence option. Anyhow, my nerves were shredded as teargas is banned in the UK, and if it was uncovered, my flight to England would certainly be over before it had begun!

Michelle inadvertently saved the day because she became a little tearful during the search, probably due to the finality of our move, coupled with the separation from her family, hitting home. Fortunately, on seeing her distress the customs official stopped after the first case and sent us on our way with his best wishes. A very close call!

Michelle did not know about the teargas. She also did not know I was going to expose the government/Inkatha collusion – at least not in any detail. Again, I understand how this may seem odd to others, but I felt it was safer all round if I did not involve Michelle directly in my activities whilst, of course, conceding that obviously she would be affected by my actions.

London in April 1991 was in the grip of a massive recession. The housing market had virtually collapsed, and the unemployment rate was at a record high. Our first priorities were to find work and accommodation. Initially then, the Inkatha exposé was put on hold.

With my background in the security industry, I was able to obtain work within the first couple of days, initially as a static guard with Securiplan before being 'promoted' to mobile inspector a couple of days later. Michelle had also found employment in London working as a personal assistant for BUPA, one of the UK's leading medical insurance companies.

Someone in Michelle's office told her that Sevenoaks was a great place to live so we hopped on a train and conducted a 'recce'. They were right. It is a beautiful town in the Kent countryside, yet within a reasonable commute of London. In addition, we found the people to be extremely friendly and welcoming. So we moved there.

Although Sevenoaks was great, these were still tough times. My day began at 04h00 in the morning when I would stumble out of bed and walk through the deserted and freezing streets of Sevenoaks to the station to catch the 05h00 train for Charing Cross. From there I had to catch two separate trains to reach the office at Golders Green for a 06h00 start. Upon completion of the standard 12 hour shift I began the return trek home where I would arrive somewhere between 20h00 and 21h00, depending on the state of London transport, have supper and go to bed before repeating the process the following day. I kept thinking to myself, 'What the hell am I doing here?'

To make things worse, our work schedules meant that Michelle and I saw very little of each other. We often had to make do with brief encounters at Charing Cross Station as I headed home after nightshift and she headed off to work.

Appropriately, my initial assignments with Securiplan brought me into contact with British Intelligence and numerous European Heads of State, and it has to be said, it was certainly not the most auspicious of introductions! After the completion of a supposedly 'comprehensive' two-day Security Course at Securiplan headquarters, the fourteen or so 'graduates', most of whom couldn't spell security let alone enforce it, were unleashed on the International Maritime Organisation Headquarters as part of the protective measures for a meeting of European Heads of State.

It was like something out of 'Police Academy'! Two days' training! No intelligence agency could have vetted the people on the course in that time. London in the early 90s was the favourite target of the IRA, yet the security was so slack that fourteen likely lads could gain unrestricted access to a building hosting a major convention. This was contrary to any protection procedures I had studied.

On the first day of the conference I got to within a foot of British Prime Minister John Major when I opened the door for him to the main conference area. Worse still, security staff did not search the belongings of Securiplan officers, allowing them to pass their bags around the X-Ray machines! I just could not believe what I was seeing! I'm glad to say that my later experiences with the MI5 and MI6 revealed a far greater professionalism.

Once established in job and home, and with some money coming in, it was time to release the documents. In my naivety, odd after so long in the SB, I hoped to expose the covert Inkatha/government alliance, damage the regime and assist the ANC without my involvement becoming public knowledge. That was the plan. It seemed so simple at the time, but turned out to be much harder than I thought.

In retrospect, I think we could have avoided the harsh reality of our lives during this period if I had followed the mercenary approach of others. It would have been considerably easier, and maybe smarter, to head straight to Fleet Street with the information, sell my story to the highest bidder and then sit back and accept the plaudits that would certainly have come my way. I could have written the headlines myself: 'Privileged white South African risks all for justice and truth!' In retrospect, it would have been the smart thing to do but it never crossed my mind to look for personal profit or gain. I viewed it as 'blood money'.

I thought about going to the ANC. I could have made a beeline for the ANC London offices with my cache of documents where I'm sure I would have been welcomed with open arms. Consider the furore surrounding Dirk Coetzee at the time and the way in which the ANC went out of their way to support him – now there is a great role model! However, I never considered the ANC a viable option since they had been so successfully penetrated with apartheid agents that I could just as likely be handing the documents back to the government! After all I had been through to get them, I was not going to let that happen.

Instead, I wanted to make contact with any one of a number of journalists that I had identified who would then arrange for the publication of the Inkatha story. However, this proved easier said than done, partly due to my own incompetence, and partly due to the incompetence of the journalists I contacted.

Wanting to remain incognito was a major restriction, as was the issue of who to trust. By my reckoning, the options available were fairly limited, with only the *Guardian* and the *Independent* newspapers adopting a consistent anti-apartheid, one-person-one-vote line in their editorial content.

My first port of call was John Carlin, the Africa correspondent of the *Independent*, whose columns I had followed in South Africa and who appeared to have the necessary credentials to make full use of the information. (I later worked with Carlin as part of a BBC Assignment Programme on the third force.) However, he missed out on the Inkathagate scoop as he would not agree to a face-to-face meeting in London but rather wanted me to fax the documents to him in South Africa. He was too busy covering the visit of Margaret Thatcher to South Africa, which was big news at the time. His loss!

I next approached Carlin's London-based colleague, the African Affairs editor Richard Dowden, providing a detailed synopsis of the information at my disposal during a lengthy telephone conversation to which he replied, 'Well, it seems fairly interesting but unfortunately I'm about to head off on leave and am not in a position to follow up on the story.' Good thing Woodward and Bernstein (the reporters who broke the Watergate scandal) weren't due a vacation, hey! Such dedication! Strike two!

My breakthrough came when I contacted David Beresford, the South African *Guardian* correspondent, who agreed to a meeting in a Soho pub in London. In the best traditions of espionage, we agreed that he would wear a red shirt so I could recognise him, as obviously neither of us knew each other from a bar of soap. Of course, the pub could have been full of people wearing red… but at least it was a start.

At the meeting, I revealed the top secret files in my possession, outlining for the first time concrete proof of government support for Inkatha. Of course the documents meant little to him in themselves as they were all in Afrikaans, but I outlined their contents over the duration of the meeting. It should be noted that I was attempting to establish these contacts in between working twelve-hour shifts, often on a rotating shift roster. These were very hectic times.

Thankfully, Beresford decided to run with the story. I was impressed and, I have to admit, a little relieved that Beresford had agreed to meet me given that he only knew me as 'Andy' and had virtually no knowledge as to my occupation and history. Equally, what did he have to lose? If it turned out to be a wild goose chase, all he would have wasted was one afternoon of his life and a few pounds of the *Guardian*'s expense account!

Throughout the meeting, particularly as the impact of the potential exposé began to dawn on him, he kept asking 'but what do you get out of it?' as though it was impossible to imagine that someone would do this without asking for some kind of reward or favour. I assured him that all I wanted was the truth to be published and for the South African and world public to have the luxury of making up their own minds.

As it was, the subsequent exposure made worldwide news, but with hindsight, it would have been even bigger if I had provided a face and a human interest aspect to the scandal, because I could have ensured that the right questions were asked, since in many ways, the government managed to slip off the hook that I had baited.

There are a number of issues that should have been handled more competently by the newspapers. Why the big rush to print? Because they could not believe their luck at the size of the story that had fallen into their hands! With a little more composure they could easily have taken their time to check dates and the alibis of the key individuals mentioned in the documents instead of rushing in head-first.

For example, how difficult would it have been to tail Major Louis Botha and Buthelezi to confirm the existence of a relationship? This provided Buthelezi, in particular, with the opportunity to shift blame to his subordinates. Furthermore, there was absolutely no attempt to explore the information I had provided relating to the existence of Askari farms in Natal and other regions. At this time, the press and public were still labouring under the misapprehension that Vlakplaas was the one and only base for Askaris. Every province had at least one, yet this was not even mentioned in the disclosures. Other information, such as the police involvement in explosions, either as a result of 'dirty tricks' or cover for Askaris on the payroll, failed to receive a mention.

Basically, the press uncovered no significant evidence in addition to the documents I provided. I was the Inkathagate scandal, so to speak. Indeed, this is a fundamental reason for this book. You only have to study the press reports of the time to identify that the documentation I provided was the sole basis for the revelations. In addition, it is often overlooked that I provided the documentary proof for the funding of UWUSA as well as for the state funding of the National Students Federation.

The *Weekly Mail* deliberately released the information over a number of weeks to maximise its newsworthy impact, not because they 'uncovered' the information over time. They were in the possession of all the information from day one. This tactic did prove reasonably effective in that the government stumbled from one public relations disaster to another as the *Weekly Mail* editor in South Africa, Anton Harber, knew exactly what buttons to push.

But back to the meeting with Beresford. He asked for a couple of days to corroborate my story before a subsequent meeting took place where I somewhat reluctantly allowed him to photocopy the documents in my possession. My reluctance was not so much about me not trusting Beresford, as about the enormity of what was to follow. Deep down I knew this was a life-changing moment. And all it amounted to was handing over the documents and walking away – and the rest, as they say, is history.

Working in collaboration with Anton Harber, Beresford coordinated a simultaneous worldwide release of the scoop for Friday 19 July 1991. In a discussion I had with Beresford a number of years later he said he would not have agreed to the joint release had he realised how big the story was to become.

The day the story broke is etched in my memory. Michelle and I were on our way to our respective jobs when I bought the *Guardian* at Charing Cross Station. All along, I think Michelle was of the opinion that I had exaggerated the impact of the story, but it still came as a shock to both of us to see the headline on the front page, not to mention all the newspaper billboards in the station: 'South African police cash went to Inkatha.' Unbeknown to us of course, the *Weekly Mail* in South Africa broke the news with the headline 'Police paid Inkatha to block ANC', together with the statement 'Remarkable documents tell of police payments to Inkatha'.

The weekend following the release of the scandal was extremely tense and surreal, but I looked at the coverage and its dramatic impact with a sense of pride. I had achieved my aim of exposing the duplicity and callous nature of the National Party government and Buthelezi's IFP. The scandal took on a momentum of its own, being the lead item on both the ITV and BBC television news and with the *Guardian's* rival broadsheets getting in on the action. Anthony Sampson, author of *Mandela: The Authorised Biography*, wrote of the scandal, 'Rarely has any news story had such an immediate impact on a government'.

Press coverage continued unabated in the weeks after the story broke as the true extent and depth of the funding became clear. Ministers, most notably Adriaan Vlok and Pik Botha, were at sixes and sevens since their lies and deceptions were exposed on national TV.

*The paper for a changing South Africa*

# THE WEEKLY MAIL

R2,20 (R1,95 + 25c GST) ★Southern Africa: R2,20 excl. t

Volume 7, Number 28. July 19 to July 25 1991

**TOM SHARPE comes back after 30 years**
The much-banned satirist returns to SA to speak at the Mail Book Week PAGE 25

**The bridge that leads to nowhere**
Is there a hidden agenda behind the expensive new bridge? PAGE 10

**Judges join the outcry over released prisoners** PAGE 8

Two terse sentences that betray a political scandal ...

MASSA VERGADERING : INKATHA : KINGSPARK, DURBAN : 1990-03-25

1. Hierby aangeheg kwitansie vir die bedrag van R150,000-00.

A two-line memo from Natal security police headquarters, confirming payment of R150 000 to Inkatha for organising a rally

WEEKLY MAIL SPECIAL INVESTIGATION

Remarkable documents tell of police payments to Inkatha

# *Police paid Inkatha to block ANC*

By EDDIE KOCH and ANTON HARBER

THE South African Police have paid large amounts of money to help Inkatha oppose the African National Congress.

*The Weekly Mail* has also obtained copies of internal security police documents showing extensive discussions between Inkatha president Chief Mangosuthu Buthelezi and a senior Durban security policeman about ways of preventing the ANC from eroding Inkatha's support in Natal.

At least R250 000 was paid into an Inkatha bank account by the security police for the purpose of organising rallies and other anti-ANC activities shortly after the release from prison of ANC president Nelson Mandela. One rally paid for by the SAP, at King's Park, Durban on March 25 1990, was the spark for an upsurge in civic violence that has come to be known as the Maritzburg War".

According to a top-secret security police memorandum, Buthelezi was very emotional and expressed extreme gratitude for the extent of the financial assistance provided.

The documents reveal that Buthelezi was concerned about declining membership figures in Natal at the time of Mandela's release from prison and had serious misgivings about the support of some of Inkatha's key leaders, including Inkatha chairman Frank Mdlalose and former secretary general Oscar Dhlomo.

*The Weekly Mail* has receipts, First National Bank deposit slips, and internal security police memoranda, marked "Top Secret/Uiters Geheim", which confirm the police payments to Inkatha as well as face-to-face meetings between Buthelezi, some of his cabinet ministers, and Major Louis Botha, senior officer in the Durban regional security police, to discuss how to deal with the ANC.

In a 10-page memorandum to the chief of security police in Pretoria, dated February 13 1990 (number S7/28/3/8/4n), Botha asks for R120 000 because it was of "cardinal importance" that arrangements were made for a massive turnout at an Inkatha rally "to show everyone that he (Buthelezi) has a strong base".

"It is recommended that a clandestine grant of at least R120 000 be made available for this purpose," Botha wrote to his superiors. "It should also be accepted that Inkatha does not have the financial means to arrange such a gathering on its own. The consequences of this rally failing will have far-reaching implications for Buthelezi and the RSA."

Further letters and receipts show that this payment was made in hard cash into an account in the name of Inkatha/Kgare (Kgare is the organisation's Sotho name) at First National Bank in Durban on March 15, 10 days before the rally. The account number was 221426-8006961533.

The security branch of the police has since been disbanded but it is widely believed that its officers are still deployed for covert political operations.

*The Weekly Mail* also has confirmation of a payment of R100 000 to Inkatha to organise another rally on November 5 1989. The rally was in fact held on November 19 and was addressed by King Goodwill Zwelithini.

This document, a letter from Brigadier JA Steyn, deputy regional chief of the security police in Natal, to the commanding officer of the security police in Pretoria, says that Buthelezi and his justice minister, Jeffrey Mtetwa, asked that their "thanks and great appreciation be passed on to those responsible for passing on the funds.

"Chief Minister Buthelezi was very emotional when a copy of the receipt was given to him. He could not say thank you enough and said that he had not expected it."

*The Weekly Mail*, working in conjunction with *The Guardian* of London, has run extensive checks on the documents. It has confirmed the Inkatha bank account numbers, the identities, addresses and telephone numbers of all those named in them, and the details of the Durban rallies.

There is no conclusive evidence that Buthelezi or members of Inkatha knew that the money deposited into their account came directly from the security police.

Botha is well known in Durban as a security policeman with close links to Inkatha and at the time of the documentation was often seen in Buthelezi's company. In the words of one source, "wherever Buthelezi was, Botha was".

●To PAGE 3

NEXT WEEK IN THE WEEKLY MAIL: A SPECIAL FOCUS ON THE ENVIRONMENT

# In full: The ten page memo from Major Botha

**The full Afrikaans text of the memo from Major Louis Botha of the Durban security police, to the head of the security police in Pretoria, concerning a major Inkatha rally in March last year**

Major L Botha
Kantoor van die Streekhof
Veiligheidstak
Privaatsak X54320 Durban 4000
031-322322 X 426
1990-02-13

Die Hoof Veiligheidstak
Privaatsak X302
Pretoria

MASSA VERGADERING: INKATHA: KINGS PARK: DURBAN: 1990-03-25

1. Telefoniese gesprek tussen kaptein KOEKEMOER (B3) en majoor L BOTHA van Natal Streek op 1990-02-12 asook hierdie Streek se faksberignommer 118 gedateer 1990-02-08 met verwysing S22/29/12 het betrekking.
2. Oor die afgelope 2/3 weke het verskeie vertroulike gesprekke tussen hoofminister MG BUTHELEZI en majoor L BOTHA oor die INKATHA/UDF/MDM/ANC stryd plaasgevind. Tydens van hierdie gesprekke het hoofminister BUTHELEZI sy hope en vrese ten opsigte van die ANC ook uitgespreek. Hierdie Streek het dit nodig geag dat VHK ingelig moet word.
3. Dit is 'n bekende feit en verslae is reeds daaroor gelewer, dat Hoofminister BUTHELEZI 'n ondersteuner van die ANC is, dog verwerp hy sekere aspekte van die ANC beleid. Sy houding veral ten opsigte van geweld met die gepaardgaande implikasies, sy teenkanting van die sanksies en disinvesterings veldtog en sy verwerping van sosialisme (beleid van die ANC) is drie baie belangrike aspekte wat 'n wig tussen hom (en dan INKATHA) en die ANC indrywe.
4. Tydens die gesprekke het dit baie duidelik geword dat die optredes en politieke skuiwe van die ANC 'n mate van angs by die Hoofminister laat posvat veral as daar gekyk word na die kwynende INKATHA lede tal en die implikasies wat dit vir hom inhou.

4.1. Die Hoofminister is tans besig met verskeie pogings om alliansies met ander groepe te vorm, dog sonder veel sukses.

4.2. Hier word onder andere na die PAC verwys. Nadat hy die terugkeer van Prins V SHANGE oud-PAC lid bewerkstellig het, het hy gehoop dat die Zulu faksie in die PAC hom sou ondersteun maar dit het nie gerealiseer nie. (November 1989).

4.3. Net so met die terugkeer van Dr W Z CHONCO (S4/2031N).

4.4 Hy is ook betrokke met die moontlike terugkeer van Joe MATTHEWS (S4/997) in 'n poging om sy isolasie te breek en ondersteuning te verkry.

5. Dit is ook duidelik dat ten spyte van die briewe wat hy vanaf Nelson MANDELA ontvang het waarin MANDELA erkenning aan hom vir sy (BUTHELEZI) se stryd verleen, verwerp die ANC/MDM/UDF hom nog steeds.
6. Die Hoofminister is ook baie agterdogtig oor die Xhosa oorheersing binne die Nasionale Uitvoerende Komitee (NUK) van die ANC en hulle vyandige houding teenoor hom.

7.1. Dit is ook duidelik dat hy baie agterdogtig is vir toenadering van die ANC want volgens hom sal dit maklik vir die ANC hieragie wees om hom (BUTHELEZI) te vernietig as hy en INKATHA by die ANC sou aansluit. Dan trek die ANC in werklikheid 'n coup op INKATHA. Hy het ook Goven MBEKI se Stockholm verklaring (sien hierdie Streek se faksberig waarna daar in para 1 verwys is) met agterdog behandel. Luidens hom is hy ook baie kwaad oor Tom SEBINA se uitlatings in Lusaka. (Sien faksberig waarna daar in para 1 verwys word).

7.2. Hy is ook bekommerd oor die moontlike rol wat van sy ondersteuners en Kabinetslede bv
- Dr O DLOMO - Minister van Onderwys
- Dr F MDLALOSE - Minister van Gesondheid
- Inkosi GUMEDE - Minister van Openbare Werke
- Minister S SITHEBE - Minister van Binnelandse aangeleenthede,

nou sal speel (Sien hierdie Streek se verslag S22/29/16N gedateer 1989-08-23 met opskrif "KONFLIK BINNE INKATHA AS GEVOLG VAN DIE VREDESAMESPREKINGS" asook die memorandum "STRATEGIESE PERSPEKTIEF : HOOFMINISTER BUTHELEZI EN INKATHA : IMPLIKASIES VIR HUIDIGE ONDERHANDELINGSPOLITIEK" gedateer 1989-09-22.

7.3. Die Hoofminister het ook sy ernstige kommer uitgespreek oor die rol van die jeug in die huidige politiek. Die feit dat die jeug wat vandag geweld aanblaas en sy INKATHA lede aanval, more se kiesers sal wees, is vir hom 'n geweldige probleem en dra by tot sy onsekerheid.

8.1. Dit het baie duidelik tydens die gesprekke navore gekom dat die Hoofminister 'n onrustige periode in die politiek belewe.

8.2. As hy versoening met die ANC probeer bewerkstellig, bestaan die moontlikheid dat hy aanvaar sal word en dan van die toneel "verwyder" sal word of die ANC sal hom summier verwerp en sodoende polities vernietig. Staan hy op die "kantlyn" van die politiek, sal hy nie later aan die "spel" kan deelneem nie wat tog tot politieke vernedering sal lei, (al dus die Hoofminister).

8.3. In die interim periode word sy politieke basis verbrokkel en kan hy nie te lank wag om 'n spesifieke rigting in te slaan nie.

8.4. KOMMENTAAR : majoor L BOTHA

8.4.1. Dit is hierdie Streek se vrees dat met die voorafgaande in gedagte, sou die Hoofminister dalk oorweeg om sy lot wel met die ANC met verreikende implikasies vir Natal en die RSA.

8.4.2. Met die vrylating van Nelson MANDELA het hierdie moontlikheid egter 'n ernigste knou opgedoen.

9. Soos alom bekend het die Hoofminister hom as jare vir onder andere die vrylating van Nelson MANDELA beywer. Hy beskou Nelson MANDELA as 'n leier en 'n Staatsman van besondere hoë gehalte. MANDELA sou vrede kon bewerkstellig en onder andere die geweld en sanksies beëindig.
10. Net voor sy TV onderhoud op 1990-02-08 te Durban waartydens hy, Minister R BOTHA en Tabo MBEKI gelyktydig opgetree het, het Hoofminister BUTHELEZI weer gemeld dat hy uitsien na Nelson MANDELA en met groot lof oor die Staats President se toespraak van 1990-02-02 gepraat. Hy het herhaaldelik gesê dat sy posisie vis-a-vis die Staats President en onderhandelings geregverdig was ten spyte van die politieke aanvalle op hom uit linkse kringe.
11. Die Hoofminister het nou planne begin beraam om 'n reeks politieke vergaderings in Natal te hou en sodoende sy politieke basis te versterk.
12. Na die vrylating van Nelson MANDELA op Sondag, 1990-02-11 het Hoofminster BUTHELEZI in 'n telefoniese gesprek met majoor BOTHA sy opgewondenheid en dankbaarheid oor die gebeure te Paarl uitgespreek. Hy het weereens die Staats President geloof vir sy politieke durf en gesê dat vrede nou binnelands bewerkstellig sal kan word.

13.1. In 'n lang gesprek van byna 'n uur en half met majoor BOTHA op 1990-02-12, het Hoofminister BUTHELEZI sy groot skok, teleurstelling en afkeur van Nelson MANDELA se openbare toespraak te Kaapstad wat hy net na sy vrylating gemaak het, uitgespreek.

13.2. In Hoofminister BUTHELEZI se eie woorde "I was shocked rigid, rendered almost speechless by the tactless unstatesmanlike speech Nelson MANDELA made".

13.3. Hier het die Hoofminister in besonder na die gedeelte van die toespraak wat soos volg gelei het "continuance of the armed struggle, the tightening of sanctions and the nationalisation of the mines, banks and large firms" verwys. Luidens Hoofminister BUTHELEZI het hy Sondag-aand baie sleg geslaap en steeds erg neerslagtig voel.

13.4. Hy maak die stelling dat Nelson MANDELA vir die Staats President beledig het en dat die Konserwatiewe Party "laughed all the way to the proverbial political bank".

13.5. Wat die posisie vererger het, aldus die Hoofminister, is die *verdere* openbare verklarings van Nelson MANDELA waarin hy weer die ANC totaal in hulle beleid ondersteun — veral die ten opsigte van die gewapende stryd, sanksies en nasionalisering van myne, ens — drie elemente wat hy geheel en al verwerp.

14. Die Hoofminister spreek sy ernstige kommer uit oor die geweld wat landswyd na die vrylating van Nelson MANDELA uitgebreek het, en die verdere verpolitisering wat plaasvind en gaan plaasvind as gevolg van verskeie optogte, vergaderings, samesprekings en media onderhoude wat die ANC/MDM/UDF beoog. Die persepsie word gevorm en versterk dat byna al die swartes (en baie blankes, Indiërs en Kleurlinge) die ANC/MDM/UDF ondersteun. Hierdie skewe beeld word dan na die wêreld uitgedra as feite. Hierdie skewe beeld van "ondersteuning" word dan gebruik in die buiteland om druk op die RSA (en INKATHA) tydens onderhandelinge te plaas.
15. As 'n teenvoeter vir hierdie eensydige propaganda en vergaderings is die Hoofminister tans besig om 'n massa INKATHA vergadering vir Kings Park, Durban vir 1990-03-25 te beplan. Huidig is daar nog 'n probleem om die stadium vir hierdie datum te bekom dog sal dit teen 1990-02-15 opgeklaar wees.
16. Die tema van die vergadering sal anti-geweld, anti-sanksies, pro-evolusioneer wees en 'n boodskap aan die RSA en die buiteland uitdra dat daar binne die RSA 'n groot massa is wat nie die ANC/MDM/UDF ondersteun nie — veral hul beleid. Hierdie aspek hou geweldige voordele vir beide die regering en INKATHA (BUTHELEZI) in tydens enige onderhandelinge.
17. Tydens die vergadering beoog die Hoofminister ook om die voordeel van sy onderhandelings politiek, anti-geweld, anti-sanksies verder uit te beeld en die President te loof vir sy politieke visie en optredes dusver.

18 KOMMENTAAR: majoor BOTHA

18.1. Hierdie Streek voel dat dit dringend noodsaaklik is dat ons 'n finansiële bydrae by so 'n byeenkoms moet maak. Dit is van kardinale belang dat genoeg persone by Kings Park is om die Hoofminister te ondersteun en vir almal te wys dat hy wel 'n sterk basis het.

18.2. Die nagevolge van 'n vergadering wat nie geslaagd is nie, is van selfsprekend.

18.3 Die vraag moet afgevra word of ons kan bekostig (polities) om nie so 'n vergadering onderskraag nie.

●To PAGE 10

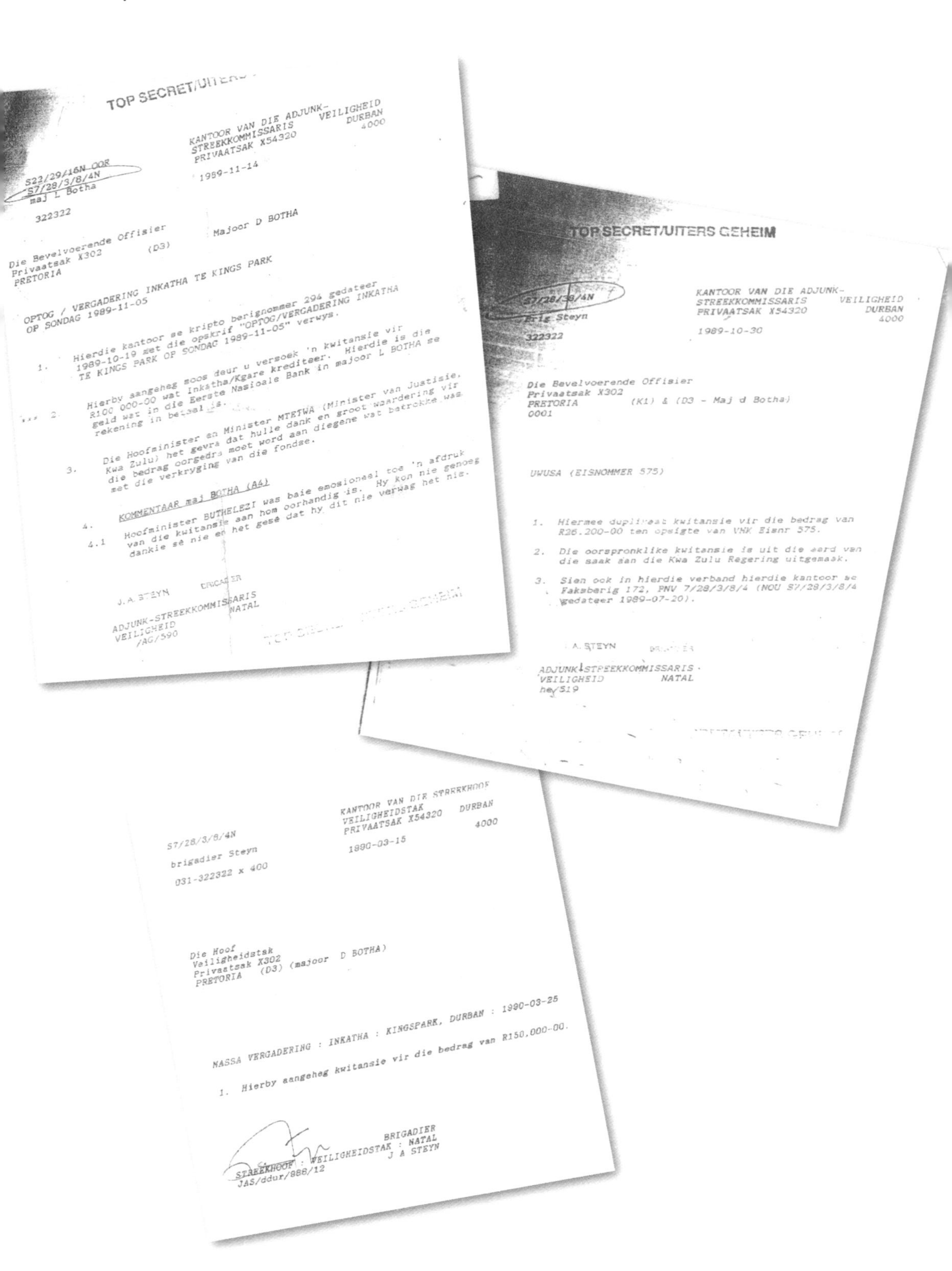

TOP SECRET/UITERS GEHEIM

KANTOOR VAN DIE ADJUNK-
STREEKKOMMISSARIS VEILIGHEID
PRIVAATSAK X54320
DURBAN
4000

1989-11-14

S22/29/16N OOR
S7/28/3/8/4N
maj L Botha

322322

Die Bevelvoerende Offisier
Privaatsak X302 (D3)
PRETORIA

Majoor D BOTHA

OPTOG / VERGADERING INKATHA TE KINGS PARK
OP SONDAG 1989-11-05

1. Hierdie kantoor se kripto berignommer 294 gedateer 1989-10-19 met die opskrif "OPTOG/VERGADERING INKATHA TE KINGS PARK OP SONDAG 1989-11-05" verwys.

2. Hierby aangeheg soos deur u versoek 'n kwitansie vir R100 000-00 wat Inkatha/Kgare krediteer. Hierdie is die geld wat in die Eerste Nasioale Bank in majoor L BOTHA se rekening in betaal is.

3. Die Hoofminister en Minister MTETWA (Minister van Justisie, Kwa Zulu) het gevra dat hulle dank en groot waardering vir die bedrag oorgedra moet word aan diegene wat betrokke was met die verkryging van die fondse.

4. KOMMENTAAR maj BOTHA (A4)

4.1 Hoofminister BUTHELEZI was baie emosioneel toe 'n afdruk van die kwitansie aan hom oorhandig is. Hy kon nie genoeg dankie sê nie en het gesê dat hy dit nie verwag het nie.

J. A. STEYN BRIGADIER

ADJUNK-STREEKKOMMISSARIS
VEILIGHEID NATAL
/AG/590

TOP SECRET/UITERS GEHEIM

---

TOP SECRET/UITERS GEHEIM

S7/28/3/8/4N
Brig Steyn
322322

KANTOOR VAN DIE ADJUNK-
STREEKKOMMISSARIS VEILIGHEID
PRIVAATSAK X54320
DURBAN
4000

1989-10-30

Die Bevelvoerende Offisier
Privaatsak X302
PRETORIA (K1) & (D3 - Maj d Botha)
0001

UWUSA (EISNOMMER 575)

1. Hiermee duplikaat kwitansie vir die bedrag van R26.200-00 ten opsigte van VHK Eisnr 575.

2. Die oorspronklike kwitansie is uit die aard van die saak aan die Kwa Zulu Regering uitgemaak.

3. Sien ook in hierdie verband hierdie kantoor se Faksberig 172, PNV 7/28/3/8/4 (NOU S7/28/3/8/4 gedateer 1989-07-20).

J. A. STEYN BRIGADIER

ADJUNK-STREEKKOMMISSARIS
VEILIGHEID NATAL
hey/519

---

KANTOOR VAN DIE STREEKHOOF
VEILIGHEIDSTAK
PRIVAATSAK X54320
DURBAN
4000

S7/28/3/8/4N
brigadier Steyn
031-322322 x 400

1990-03-15

Die Hoof
Veiligheidstak
Privaatsak X302
PRETORIA (D3) (majoor D BOTHA)

MASSA VERGADERING : INKATHA : KINGSPARK, DURBAN : 1990-03-25

1. Hierby aangeheg kwitansie vir die bedrag van R150,000-00.

BRIGADIER
STREEKHOOF : VEILIGHEIDSTAK : NATAL
J A STEYN
JAS/ddur/888/12

S7/28/3/8/4N

Office of the Regional Commisioner
Security Branch
Private Bag x54320-Durban-4000
1990-03-15

Brigadier Steyn
031-3222322-400

The Head
Security Branch
Private Bag X302
Pretoria (D3) (Major D Botha)

Mass Meeting: INKATHA:KINGSPARK, DURBAN : 1990-03-25

1) Hierby attached receipt for the amount of R 150 000

REGIONAL HEAD: SECURITY BRANCH: NATAL
J A STEYN

UITERS GEHEIM

S7/28/3/8/4

NAVRAE : MAJOOR F P R BOTHA 89-10-17
TEL : 325-3480

BESTUUR EN BEHEER : PROJEK OMEGA : OPERASIE ALPHA : BYLAES AANGEHEG

1. As gevolg van die skuldelas van die "UNITED WORKERS UNION OF SOUTH AFRICA" wat moontlik die betrokkenheid van die Ministerie van Wet en Orde kan ontbloot, is die Minister deur twee aspekte gekwel. Hierdie kwelvrae is:

1.1 Hoe 'n projek wat onder die beheer van die Suid-Afrikaanse Polisie is, toegelaat was om so te ontwikkel; en

1.2 Hoe daar beoog word om die projek vorentoe te bestuur.

'n Afdruk van die memorandum in verband met die skuldelas van UWUSA word gerieflikheidshlawe aangeheg. (Bylae A).

Top Secret

S/7/28/3/8/4

Enquiries: Major F P R Botha
Tel : 325-3480

Management and Control: Project Omega:Operation Alpha

1. As a result of the records of the "United Workers Union of South Africa" which could possibly reveal the involvement of the ministry of Law and Order" the Minister is concerned about two points:

1.1 How a project that was under the control of the South African Police was allowed to get so out of control; and

1.2 How the project is going to be managed in the future

### Comment: Anton Harber

The confrontation with Vlok on SABC on the Sunday night (22 July 1991) was critical to what happened, as it really ensured his demise as minister. He resigned that week. It is also important in that, because of the unique circumstances, it was the only time one was able to confront a minister on live TV like that. It was the first time it happened, and it has never happened since.

It was largely theatre. I wanted to take documents when I met him, but not to show him how few we actually had. You have to remember that he did not know at that point what we had. So I took the newspaper's entire legal file for the year, a formidable pile of paper and stuck the relevant documents in the middle.

At some point during the TV performance, I paged through the documents, waved one in the air (I have no idea if it was a relevant one) and proclaimed, 'You are lying, Mr Vlok, and I have the evidence'.

I think Brian is due recognition for what he did, and hopefully this book will do that. The *Weekly Mail* ran checks on Brian and his story before publishing it, but we still went to press nervous and uncertain about the authenticity and the reaction we would get. In doing so, we stuck our necks out pretty far. We played the story out over time and this led to the crucial television interview that saw the demise of Adriaan Vlok and Magnus Malan.

It's also worth remembering that Inkathagate was one of a long line of exposés of security force's illegal activities of this sort, albeit one of the most important. So the media did help, although Brian hopefully will now get the credit and recognition he deserves.

I remember playing tennis on the Saturday afternoon at the Sevenoaks Clarendon Club and having discussions with both locals and expatriate South Africans about the news. Opinions were split, with the locals expressing disquiet at the government's actions while the emigrants were more than happy to justify them. I found it very difficult to keep my mouth shut and not give the game away, particularly with the South Africans who were quite happy to base their opinions on government propaganda rather than actual evidence!

As far as the ANC was concerned, I truly believe that the revelations came as a major surprise to them and as such, they were caught somewhat off-guard by the timing. Still, this was obviously a spectacular breakthrough in terms of providing concrete proof of their numerous 'third force' allegations. The government couldn't talk their way out of this one. Extracts from ANC press releases at the time provide clear examples of how the ANC made political capital from my actions.

The revelations also allowed the ANC to put the boot into Inkatha whose political credibility as an opponent of apartheid was all but demolished by the scandal. In addition, and probably for the first time, De Klerk's image as a man of integrity was potentially tarnished abroad. In stark contrast, Nelson Mandela's international standing was elevated by the revelations.

Yet despite clearly benefiting from the scandal (as I suppose I had intended), there remained a sense that the ANC were not well-pleased by the manner or perhaps the timing of the revelations. I think, one reason for their stance may have been identified by Australian academic Professor John Kane who wrote, 'Inkathagate embarrassed both leaders (De Klerk and Mandela) but Mandela more so since it called into question his judgement in trusting the white leader. He despised De Klerk thereafter but never doubted his continuing need for him.' In my opinion, this displeasure explains why the ANC has failed to recognise my actions subsequent to my going public in 1995.

In addition, I could never quite shake the feeling that there was a sense of outrage and disappointment in the ANC that I had not come to them with the information. I feel sure they would have handled the release of the documents quite differently, if indeed they had released them at all.

### ANC Press Statements

The damming revelations reported by the *Weekly Mail* today regarding the government's deep involvement in fuelling and perpetrating the violence that has already caused such a massive loss of black life, are cause for serious concern among all South Africans. The transformation of Natal and many parts of the reef into killing fields must be laid squarely at the door of the government. During the past six years, the ANC has repeatedly called attention to the government's apparent inability to bring the violence to an end. Today's exposé indicates that senior state officials have been directly involved in funding political activities in opposition to the ANC and bear the direct responsibility for the murder, sometimes of entire African families, in both the PWV and Natal.

...the facts that have come to light pose a grave threat to the entire peace process. They are a clear indication that the De Klerk government has been pursuing a twin-track strategy of posing as committed to peace while waging a ruthless war against the democratic movement in general and the ANC in particular. The NWC was of the unanimous view that the shocking revelations about the SADF, using foreign mercenaries to massacre South African citizens in their homes, at places of recreation and on the public transport system are inextricably connected to the multi-million rand special slush fund set up to finance Inkatha in order to shore up its sagging political fortunes as an opposition to the ANC.

...Furthermore, attention is presently focused on the manipulation of Inkatha, but this needs to be seen in the wider framework of a considered destabilisation policy by successive apartheid governments, including President De Klerk.

> The 'confession' of MZ Khumalo does not diminish the responsibility of the Inkatha leadership and Chief Buthelezi himself, we doubt that he could have been unaware of so generous a donation and its source. Minister Vlok unequivocally states that the money was accounted for in full by Inkatha officials.

In his response, De Klerk did a great job of damage limitation. Sure, he had to sacrifice two of his ministers but it could, and probably should, have been much worse. However, the covert alliance with Inkatha was broken, and the NP's election prospects damaged, so I had achieved my prime objectives. The assurances from De Klerk that there would be no further covert funding of political parties and that all such funds would be carefully accounted for were meaningless platitudes, as subsequent revelations over the years have proven.

To my amazement, Buthelezi, though obviously severely compromised, seemed to be keeping his head afloat in the face of the veritable tidal wave of evidence of collusion that was now heading in his direction. That Buthelezi could claim to know nothing of the funding, even after the government publicly admitted to it, is just laughable. To quote from a top secret memorandum by Major Louis Botha: 'Chief Minister Buthelezi was very emotional when a copy of the receipt was handed over to him. He could not say thank you enough and said that he had not expected it.' And yet the press still allowed him to claim he was unaware of the funding! I was amazed at the time. What more evidence could I be expected to provide?!

I was told this time and time again by none other than Major Louis Botha himself. At no stage has anyone questioned the accuracy of the information I provided because it was all true and verifiable. That is why the government was forced to act in the way it did and why it created such a worldwide impact. The government's actions speak for themselves!

On one level, I blame myself since, if I had been prepared to stand up in public, I could have refuted their fairly absurd claims to have been unaware of the source of the funds and the scapegoat, MZ Khumalo.

Major Louis Botha was the Security Branch's liaison officer with Chief Buthelezi and Inkatha, in addition to his role of supervising VIP protection duties in the Durban region. Botha enjoyed such a close personal relationship with Inkatha and the Chief that his nickname within the SB was 'Major Buthelezi'.

Once I had uncovered the covert SB funding of Inkatha in late 1988, I intentionally cultivated a relationship with Botha. He was an eloquent and intelligent man, particularly by SB standards. For some reason, he had taken a personal interest in me from the outset of my time at the SB, which made this easier. He seemed to enjoy our conversations on current affairs and the world in general. We developed a rapport that I manipulated in order to obtain information as to the current state of play with Inkatha and future plans whenever an opportunity presented itself.

I managed to maintain a reasonable frequency of contact with Botha as his office was located just along the corridor from mine and often, when assigned VIP duties, I found myself working in his section. Obviously this took time as I could in no way appear overly interested in the SB funding of Inkatha, particularly once documents started to disappear. In a way, I felt kind of guilty that I was taking advantage of him but I rationalised it as the end-result that justified the means.

Major Botha was firmly of the opinion that government support for Inkatha was fully justified and that, in his mind, he was acting in the best interests of his country. If you have ever read the full ten-page transcript of the memo he drafted, justifying the need for SB funding for Inkatha and Buthelezi to counter Mandela and the ANC, you will understand what I mean. The fact that this funding was illegal, covert, undemocratic and exacerbated the violence in Natal, seemed to elude him completely. (See pages 71–72 for some key points from the Botha Memorandum.)

Over and above the Botha Memorandum, there was also the evidence of the cheques identifying the SB payment for the two rallies at Kings Park and further documentary verification of payments to UWUSA, together with memoranda from the office of the Minister of Law and Order, registering concern that SB funding was not being correctly audited. The relationship was proven beyond doubt.

Once the exposé had run its course and the government effectively admitted wrongdoing, I still did not consider going public as the whistleblower. Basically, I felt a deep sense of uneasiness that my actions might force Michelle and myself to move just as we had begun to settle and develop friendships. My concerns in this regard were worsened by reports in the *Guardian* that David Beresford's home in Johannesburg had been broken into, but nothing appeared to have been taken. Strange burglars! It was obviously an attempt by the SB to identify the source of his information.

The report also stated that an ex-colleague, Sergeant Karl Eysele, had been recorded on tape by journalists giving instructions to a source to break into a retired female officer's residence (I assumed it must have been Jenny Chapman) to ascertain whether she could be the potential mole. Another article entitled 'SA Police to root out funding leaks' outlined the force's commitment to finding the perpetrator and the ten-year jail term awaiting them for contravention of the Official Secrets Act. This did little to improve my sense of humour.

My fear of being exposed was dramatically enhanced whilst working nightshift on a site-visit in central London on Thursday 25 July 1991. I happened to glance at an article concerning the Inkathagate scandal in *The Times* newspaper. I read the following lines with increasing horror:

> Meanwhile intelligence agents believe they have identified the 'deep throat' who leaked incriminating security police documents to South African and British newspapers. The suspect is said to be a policeman based in Durban, who has disappeared with secret

> files. It is understood the documents, with copies of bank accounts and receipts were released in London last week.

The only thing missing was my bloody photograph! I nearly had a nervous breakdown on the spot. Looking back now it's quite comical how I panicked, but at the time, I was truly terrified. In my defence, it has to be borne in mind that Michelle and I had no-one to turn to for support. No-one. We were on our own in a new country, working bloody long hours, making new friends and oh, leaking information about police collusion!

Imagining the worst and in a state of total panic, I rushed home to see if Michelle was okay. I don't know why, but I imagined that she might be in real danger and my first instinct was to see if she was safe. Sadly, the obvious solution of a phone call was out of the question as we did not have a home phone at this time.

Getting to Sevenoaks from central London at near midnight was no easy task, I can tell you! I had to return my patrol vehicle to North London under the pretext of a family emergency, catch the usual two tubes to Charing Cross and then an overnight train to Sevenoaks. In a panic at the station, I tried desperately to get in touch with David Beresford, the one person to whom I could at least talk, but he had left the country.

Arriving home breathless after my dash across London, I found Michelle fast asleep! What a relief! She too, was fairly aghast upon hearing that it was clear that I was the prime suspect in the scandal.

As this incident shows, fear of reprisal was the main reason for wanting to remain anonymous. I was really worried about the danger to family and friends who remained behind in SA, while I lay secure (or so I believed at the time) in the United Kingdom.

My entire upbringing revolved around a sense of responsibility and doing the right thing. One has to remember that this was 1991 and the political and security scene was extremely volatile, particularly in Natal. I imagined my parents' business being petrol-bombed or a parcel bomb in the post. The TRC showed that these fears were well-grounded.

Actually, this was the one area where I feel Beresford let me down. I specifically requested him to act as if he had received the documents in South Africa, which would have widened the prospective number of sources, deflecting attention away from myself, although I realised that I would always be a potential suspect. News reports on the BBC over the twenty-four hour period after the story broke made it perfectly clear that the information had been obtained in London and from then on it was really only going to be a matter of time before I became the obvious candidate.

In fact, I had already been identified as the key suspect in the theft of the documents since threatening letters had already been sent to both my parents and in-laws, outlining my culpability in the scandal and what I could expect if I dared to return.

**Threatening letter to in-laws:**

Mr J Smith
36 Glenwood Avenue
Malvern
Durban

Sir

We have proof that Brian Morrow was responsible for the theft of documents which led to the Inkathagate scandal. This not only had far-reaching political repercussions but also damaged the economy tremendously.

The coward could not even face up to his actions, but deserted the country which has given him so much.

The damage to our country will remain long after he has spent the 'few gold coins' he received.

We have conveyed this information to the police but they seem incapable of doing anything about him.

We therefore undertake –

- to enforce law and order [by ourselves]
- to see to it that the traitor Brian Morrow receives his just rewards if he ever returns to this country

Unfortunately your daughter has been tainted by the actions of her husband, although we know her to be innocent.

You can imagine how happy my parents-in-law would have been reading that. Just what you want! Your daughter marrying a traitor! I have always been amused by the SB's acknowledgement of Michelle's innocence. That's one thing they got right. Again, all production credit had to go to the SB, probably Graham Jordan, though with some assistance as the emotive language was fairly well crafted and way beyond his usual standard.

It says more about them than me that they could not envisage someone doing something altruistically but have to assume that 'I did it for money'. It is something that rankles me to this day and an issue that I want to make absolutely clear. I neither asked for nor received a single cent at any stage of the revelations, including the 'work' I did for British Intelligence.

In the event, I was blissfully unaware of these threatening letters at the time because my family kept their existence to themselves until 1995 when I applied for indemnity. This was the standard practice in both families where there was little support or understanding for what I had done, with the notable exception of my father. In fact, strange as though this may seem, to this day the topic has never been raised. It is simply not up for discussion. This is in no way a criticism, just a realistic appraisal of the facts. They, of course, had never been party to the plan and I lived in the belief that they were totally unaware of my involvement.

So, I decided to move on with my life. I had always wanted to try my hand at teaching and managed to get a job at a private school in Blackheath, South London, thanks to my primary degree and 'life experience' – such as it was! I taught Years Six to Eight with a little GCSE History thrown in. Anyhow, just after I settled into the new job and began to feel normal again, fate once again played its hand.

One evening, whilst watching television, there was a knock on the door. Michelle and I looked at each other wondering who it could be, as we were not expecting company and it was probably around 21h00. Upon opening the door a complete stranger asked if this was the home of Brian Morrow, the man responsible for leaking the documents that had led to the Inkathagate scandal!

What the hell do you say to that? In my mind only three people in the world knew that I had stolen the documents. And two of them were Michelle and me! Had Beresford betrayed my confidence? However, even that line of thought had its complications. When I met Beresford, he had no knowledge of my name, address or occupation and I had changed jobs since our last meeting. How the hell had this guy found me? I decided that the only course of action was to invite him in out of the cold and rain as I was keen to elicit some information of my own.

He introduced himself as John Drury, the BBC producer of the Assignment series shown on BBC2, a sort of lesser-known Panorama, currently engaged in the production of a documentary on the violence in South Africa, focusing on government collaboration in so-called third force activities. Drury said that he had received information that I was the source of the Inkathagate scandal and asked if I was interested in appearing in the documentary together with providing background information wherever possible. Although I pressed him hard, he would not reveal his source, and actually never did, despite my best efforts. Subsequent events made me suspect intelligence involvement though.

After several meetings, I acknowledged my involvement in the scandal and agreed to assist in any way that I could. It was a project that I wholeheartedly supported since I saw it as another opportunity to expose government corruption and collusion in the violence in South Africa. Despite numerous requests, I refused to be interviewed on the programme – basically for fear of reprisals.

And once again, my fears had some foundation. One morning, just before I was due to leave for school Michelle received a phone call from a man who declined to leave his name but specifically asked to speak to Brian. He had phoned the day before but I had already left. The second phone call was bizarre, not least because

Michelle was in the room listening and I did not want to alarm her, so I could not engage in dialogue to the extent that I would have liked.

In essence the man (with a heavy Afrikaans accent) claimed to be from the South African Intelligence community and he just wanted to inform me that I should cease my involvement in the proposed BBC third-force documentary or I would come to serious harm. Inkathagate had been bad enough, but any further involvement would have dire consequences. He then proceeded to give a remarkably detailed, and terrifyingly accurate, account of both my wife and my movements over the previous weekend.

You can imagine how happy this made me feel! I replayed the conversation over and over in my mind on the long commute to school; my mind a whirl of emotions. Again Michelle and I had no-one to turn to. Our lives were being threatened yet we had to carry on with our careers and relationships as if nothing was wrong. We were ordinary people caught up in extraordinary events, although admittedly of my own making. I presumed that we had been followed by agents from the South African Embassy in London. From then on we resolved to be extra-vigilant in our everyday lives.

Clearly, the SB feared I might have evidence of other government skulduggery. Further, Drury and Carlin were themselves victims of SB harassment at this time, the most newsworthy incident being the attempt to frame Drury upon his return to the UK from South Africa.

Acting on an 'anonymous tip', the police detained Drury upon his arrival at Heathrow where an examination of his luggage revealed a cache of four bags of cannabis and a dozen Mandrax tablets. He was held for nine hours before being released without charge at the behest of British government officials. The assumption was that the SB had planted the evidence in his luggage at Jan Smuts Airport in Johannesburg in an attempt to discredit his journalistic integrity and possibly 'persuade' him not to continue with the documentary. This incident was given front page coverage in the *Independent* on Thursday 5 March 1992 under the headline 'South African security services harass British journalists'.

This was not the first time that Drury had found himself in hot water at a South African airport. In one of our conversations I had mentioned to him that my work briefcase probably still contained several incriminating documents, including one with evidence that De Klerk himself had congratulated certain NSF members on the success of their activities.

I informed my father-in-law that a friend from the UK was going to pick up the briefcase while on a visit to Durban. Heaven knows what my father-in-law thought of all of this, but I was completely unaware that he knew of my involvement in the scandal. The case probably did contain several important documents, the most valuable being the duty roster containing the names, section and call-sign of every Durban SB member.

Upon leaving Durban's airport, Drury found himself the centre of some unwanted attention when the metal detector went off as he passed through. Upon searching his briefcase the police were surprised to find over 50 rounds of 9mm ammunition that I had forgotten in the case! I don't know why he didn't open it before he boarded the plane!

This was of course way before the days of Al Qaeda and Drury managed to smooth-talk his way out of the situation – minus the rounds of course. I never saw either my briefcase or its contents again, but at the time, I was fairly certain that they had found a new home at British Intelligence. It appeared strange that he had returned but didn't hand back my briefcase or discuss the contents with me. Owing to the circumstances of the time I didn't push the issue with him.

I'm not sure of Drury's relationship with British Intelligence, but the evidence would certainly seem to indicate some form of liaison on the part of either Drury or Carlin. How else would you explain the appearance of the SB and the disappearance of my suitcase?

I arrived at the decision to contact John Carlin and John Drury who were in South Africa conducting interviews and research for the forthcoming documentary. In fact, their investigations had almost certainly led to the phone call. At some point, one of them must have mentioned my name, either on the phone (many were tapped) or in a conversation with a potential informant.

Eventually, I managed to get through to them at their Durban hotel and relayed the contents of the phone conversation. My concerns must have struck a chord, and almost certainly indicated who one or both of them worked for on the side, because a couple of days later I had two more late evening visitors…

This time, they introduced themselves at the door as British Special Branch members, complete with flash ID badges, and enquired whether anyone had made threats against my life. Now, this again came out of the blue, since neither Carlin nor Drury had warned me to expect any assistance from the police, let alone the Special Branch! Life certainly wasn't dull!

I was extremely glad to see them and it certainly helped put our minds at ease. At the very least, we could voice our concerns and have someone to talk to. We didn't need to pretend all the time. Michelle appeared particularly reassured by their presence. They informed us that the local Sevenoaks Police Station had been notified of our circumstances and that patrols would routinely cover our area. In addition, they provided emergency contact numbers for both themselves and the station should the circumstances warrant. They arranged to meet with me on a weekly basis, thus laying the foundations for my ultimate involvement with the British Intelligence services MI5 and MI6.

My second career as a spy had begun…

# 5

# Spy

An initial visit from Special Branch detectives in mid-1992 led to me being debriefed by British Intelligence over a period of time. The initial contact with the British Intelligence services comprised weekly meetings with the Special Branch contact, Detective Sergeant Andy Roberts. I assume there was some vetting procedure whereby my worth as a potential source was evaluated. These meetings were conducted in local parks and pubs in the Sevenoaks area. Subsequently, Andy enquired whether I had any objections to a get-together with someone with 'an interest' in my police/SB background and the South African political scene in general. At no stage were the words MI5/6 mentioned, but of course, the identity of the organisation went without saying.

I know this might sound strange for a foreign national to say, but I had no qualms whatsoever about working as a source for the British government. Their support had helped Michelle and me to retain our sanity during the entire Inkatha episode. Furthermore, I viewed this as another opportunity to expose the duplicitous nature of both the National Party and Inkatha leadership, and promote the cause of Nelson Mandela and the ANC.

It is easy, with the advantage of hindsight, to fall into the trap of assuming that Nelson Mandela and the ANC were always viewed by Western leaders as being the government-in-waiting, particularly given the iconic status Nelson Mandela went on to enjoy in the mid to late 90s and beyond, but in 1990/91 this was certainly not the case. Prior to Inkathagate, Chief Buthelezi and Inkatha had been fêted by Western heads of state as a democratic, pro-capitalist, non-violent alternative to Nelson Mandela.

I remember Margaret Thatcher praising Buthelezi, saying 'Chief minister, you and your colleagues have made an extraordinary contribution, not only in your resistance to apartheid, but also in the way you have refused to adopt that left-wing demagogic rhetoric which wins cheers and loses investment.'

British Conservative Party MP, Andrew Hunter summarised the party-view when he said, 'If a fair and just solution is to emerge in South Africa, then a platform should be provided for those black leaders, from among whose ranks will come the next black president of South Africa, so that more attention could be given to them, to men like Gatsha Buthelezi and Lucas Mangope. These men should be encouraged rather than the men of violence, the extremists and the murderers.'

It was precisely this kind of garbage about Inkatha that motivated my actions. In the late 80s and early 90s, the conservative UK government had fallen into the trap, along with other leaders in Germany and the USA, of believing that Inkatha, with its pro-capitalist, anti-sanctions and democratic posturing, offered a viable alternative to the communist-dominated ANC.

I never realised that taking vast sums of taxpayers' money, remaining callously indifferent to the genocide your policies inflicted on your people while enjoying the trappings of collaboration with the state, represented resistance to apartheid! Anyhow, Inkathagate shocked and embarrassed the British government, but to their credit, they moved swiftly to rectify the situation, and I was very happy to help them get the story straight.

In terms of content, my initial contact with what turned out to be MI6 involved a complete debriefing of everything I knew about the SB operations. This was wide-ranging and conducted professionally during numerous meetings. The topics covered ranged from structure and personnel, training procedures, courses, covert funding, collaboration, Askaris, death-squads, technology including phone-tapping, mail interception, safe houses, front companies, etc.

I suppose my major value as a source lay in the reliability of the information I could provide. Inkathagate had established my credentials and the subsequent contact with Roberts had obviously further enhanced my reputation. It quickly became apparent that MI6 had few, if any, well-placed 'assets' within the South African Intelligence community, and my appearance on the scene was considered a fairly considerable coup for the British government.

Their lack of accurate intelligence came as a surprise to me and, of course, one area where I could assist was in identifying potential sources that MI6 could approach with a view to recruitment. The line I was fed by my handlers was that there were one million potential British passport-holders in South Africa whom the

UK did not want migrating to their shores. They wanted South Africa to be as stable as possible, especially since it was one of the UK's biggest trading partners and they did not want to lose their piece of the pie. At the very least, it was considered preferable to base their foreign policy on an accurate assessment of the facts on the ground.

Contrary to the stereotype, my handlers did not bear much resemblance to 007. I had two handlers during my time with MI6, the first being James Spencer. He lasted for several years before he was reassigned and replaced with a virtual carbon copy. Both these men epitomised the stereotypical English spy with plummy public school accents and an Oxbridge education.

However, they were extremely professional, and several levels above the standard that I had experienced in the SB. I have to confess that both Michelle and I came to regard them as friends and remain grateful for their help even though, on reflection, they got more from the relationship than I did. I think it particularly suited MI6 that I was content to stay in the background and not seek publicity, unlike others who had broken ranks with the government during this time.

Other than Inkathagate, I think I was of most use to MI6 in terms of the snippets of background information I was able to provide. It is often the little insights that can be most helpful to intelligence organisations. One such example of this would be the first-hand evidence that I could provide of the National Party being genuine in its acceptance that some form of power-sharing was on the horizon and that apartheid was soon to be a thing of the past.

The SB had been privy to this information since late 1989 when all 'white' members of the SB (not a particularly auspicious start to the new era!) were instructed to attend a meeting at CR Swart Square. The corridors were abuzz with rumours as to the potential purpose of the forthcoming gathering but no one was quite prepared for what we were about to hear.

Essentially, a senior government official announced that apartheid was finished and all those present had better get used to it. Much was made of the parlous state of the South African economy and the negative impact the worldwide sanctions and trade embargoes were having on the country. Changes were on the horizon and we were told in no uncertain terms that we should prepare ourselves for them.

You can imagine that this message went down like a lead balloon! Certainly, the looks on the faces of the majority of the SB members were a sight to behold… Remember, this was some time before Nelson Mandela was freed, and I guess the government were laying the foundations for his release and the unbanning of the ANC. This was useful intelligence for the British because it provided concrete evidence that the government envisaged reform of some sort, even if they were planning to hedge their bets by a covert alliance with Inkatha.

There were also areas where I could corroborate information at their disposal or provide leads on investigations. For years my nemesis at the SB, Graham Jordan, had boasted that SB agents were responsible for the bomb attack on the ANC offices in London in 1982. Of course, I was only going on his word, but on numerous occasions he had stated that one of his old time friends, a Vic MacPherson (I think he was a major), had played a key role in the plot. He claimed that the South African Embassy in London was used as a base for the attack, with the explosives used in the strike being smuggled through customs in diplomatic bags.

Clearly, I could not provide concrete evidence to support such claims but Jordan's allegations were confirmed by testimony given at the Truth and Reconciliation Commission. Used in conjunction with other evidence, it was obvious to British Intelligence that the South African Embassy in London was a base for clandestine intelligence activity on the part of the South African government.

I also worked closely with my initial handler, James Spencer, creating profiles of policemen whom MI6 could target as potential sources for British Intelligence, identifying those who might be open to offers and eliminating others who were unlikely to play ball. Obviously, MI6 preferred their sources to be either higher up the chain of command or in an influential position. As I had illustrated with Inkathagate, working in an apparently mundane job such as filing presented a potential goldmine of information for a double agent.

I was impressed with MI6. They always conducted operations in style and in a professional manner. One 'source' operation involved the setting up of a fictional rugby tour as a pretext for making contact with the intended subject without attracting any undue attention from the South African Intelligence community. James and I met with the 'front man' for the operation, Jeffrey, at an exclusive London Club where background issues relating to the tour and the 'subject' were discussed.

Jeffery had a clean history (legend) without any obvious links to MI6, being a bona fide member of a South East London Rugby Club who had conducted tours to the area in the past. The plan required Jeffery to make telephonic contact with the target, who was an avid rugby follower in Natal, on the pretext of making arrangements for the forthcoming tour.

Such consultation would appear normal and hopefully not arouse the suspicions of the SB, particularly since they were in a heightened state of alert after the Inkathagate revelations. The target would then be required to meet another 'member' of the touring party who was conveniently in Durban on a reconnaissance mission where the offer of 'employment' would be provided. This process would not take place overnight but would follow a similar pattern to my introduction to British Intelligence.

For his efforts in setting up the potential recruitment tour leader, Jeffrey was rewarded with complimentary tickets to the forthcoming England vs South Africa

Test Match that was due to take place at Twickenham on the 14 November 1992, a game I also attended in the company of James Spencer. The guest of honour at this match was none other than President FW de Klerk, who received a standing ovation from the crowd.

It was yet another surreal moment in my life. Here I was applauding a man whom I believed was responsible for much of the bloodshed in South Africa, while standing next to a MI6 agent whose task in life was to obtain as much information concerning his government by any means possible. It's certainly a strange world!

I would like to place it on record once again that I neither asked for nor received any remuneration for my involvement with the British Security Services, unless you count some travel expenses, the odd beer and meal, and a test match as payment. I probably shelled out more cash on them than they spent on me. I helped because I felt it was the right thing to do and did not in any way see it as a betrayal of my country. It was all part of helping to bring about an end to apartheid.

My sense is that British Intelligence preferred remuneration to take the form of inducements 'in kind' rather than cash payments. In addition, when cash did change hands they did not appear to be hamstrung by the requirement for a receipt that was often the downfall of sources back in South Africa. Once a source signed a payment receipt there was no way back. They were vulnerable to blackmail from their handler who could threaten exposure if they refused to cooperate.

I honestly don't know if the 'rugby tour' operation was successful. As I have already stated, in my experience MI6 were extremely professional and certainly applied the 'need to know' intelligence mantra with much greater zeal than the SB. I was only privy to information that impacted on my role in the operation.

I'm not sure if MI6 still has informants in the South African intelligence community, but I would presume so. Inkathagate came as a rude awakening and snapped MI6 out of their complacency. Concerted efforts were made to improve both the number and quality of sources at their disposal within the South African government and its various state departments.

At first, I was not worried that working with MI6 might put me or my family back home in danger. I thought secrecy would keep me safe. But then things changed. On 15 July 1992, the *Independent* newspaper published a world exclusive outlining the existence of a South African Intelligence plot to assassinate the former South African Police Security Branch defector Dirk Coetzee, a self-confessed callous murderer who only jumped ship to save his own skin, under the headline 'Agents on mission to kill'. What was not made public was that my name was also on the list of targets for assassination.

Events transpired as follows. In early April 1992, the British Intelligence received a tip-off from a source in the South African Police that two South African agents were due to enter the United Kingdom on an unspecified mission. The individuals were identified as Captain Pamela du Randt from Military Intelligence and Leon Flores, an ex-policeman with links to the South African Intelligence community. Following up on the information, the MI5 and Special Branch (it's worth noting that MI5 and 6 don't possess the power of arrest, hence the requirement for a police presence via the Special Branch) kept Flores and Du Randt under constant surveillance from the moment they stepped off the plane at Heathrow Airport on 11 April 1992.

Having booked into the Bloomsbury Hotel in London, Flores and Du Randt made contact with Ulster Loyalists at the Three Kings Pub in West London where the details of the hits were discussed. There had been a history of complicity between the Loyalists and the South African Intelligence agencies, going back a number of years and relating mainly to the acquisition of weaponry, but the sub-contracting of 'hits' added a new dimension to the relationship. British Intelligence monitored the movements of the agents for a number of days before finally arresting them on 15 April 1992. They interrogated the pair for three days, during which Du Randt and Flores denied the existence of a 'death plot', claiming that the reason for their visit was to investigate alleged links between the IRA and the ANC.

Although there was a fairly strong circumstantial case, the decision was taken to deport the two agents rather than prosecute them for their actions. However, this served as a warning as to what lengths some elements within the South African Security establishment were prepared to go. The British government made urgent representations to the South African government, including President De Klerk himself, on this matter. An internal investigation established that the ultimate responsibility for the plot lay with the South African Police. No shocks there!

Note that we did not adopt any precautions during the assassination attempt because we knew nothing about it. Once again, all this had taken place without our knowledge, with our contact James Spencer only filling us in on the sequence of events once the pair had been detained.

The reason was simple. British Intelligence clearly felt there was no need to concern us because they placed the agents under constant surveillance. In their eyes, they had the situation under control. He said he did not want us to worry ourselves unduly! I would go even further and allege that he only informed us since he knew that the press would eventually get hold of the scoop, and that I would have experienced a nervous breakdown had I read the July headline without any background knowledge of the story.

Again, it is worth repeating that MI6 appeared very content that I appeared to have no interest in going public, unlike our friend Dirk Coetzee who milked all the publicity from the event that was humanly possible. In fact, Spencer said that the *Independent* was very keen to speak to other individuals on the 'list' and he went out of his way to assure us that we were safe and our policy of keeping a low profile was the best option available. Once again, the story was broken by my old friends

John Carlin and Richard Dowden, who must have returned from vacation refreshed and revitalised!

You can only imagine how exposed and vulnerable Michelle and I felt as we carried on with our everyday lives desperately maintaining a façade of normality, yet all the while knowing that somewhere out there people could well be plotting to kill us.

In the event, we discovered they were actually keeping an eye on us. A discovery we made in a somewhat unusual manner. As you know, I am a huge Newcastle United fan. Whilst attending a match against Chelsea in 1992, we had the misfortune to be seated in front of a group of Neanderthal Chelsea 'fans' (unfortunately Chelsea had booked us into the incorrect seating area) who were not there for the football.

As I never wore club colours to a football game they were totally unaware that I was supporting Newcastle – a good thing too as the first words I heard uttered were 'I'm gonna kill the first fucking Geordie cunt I see'. Great stuff. I do seem to have a habit of attracting trouble!

I had no intention of showing my true affinity whatsoever. However, Michelle found their constant foul language a problem and made the mistake of politely asking if they could tone it down a bit. Well, it was like a red rag to a bull and they upped the 'ante'!

Then Chelsea scored. No problem. I stood up to clap, masking my inner disappointment, but the group behind went crazy, with one of them knocking Michelle down in his exuberance and then refusing to get off her. He would have weighed over 100kgs and, as he would not move voluntarily I 'helped' him off.

Well, that started the fireworks! All seven yobbos climbed into me, which led to the police stepping in with batons drawn. Michelle had come off worst in the scuffle, with blood dripping down her face. The police made several arrests and we all missed the second half when we were carted off to the Kensington Police Station. As if our lives weren't complicated enough! After taking our statements we were released and, somewhat wearily, made our way back home to Sevenoaks.

The next day, none other than MI6 operative James Spencer appeared on our doorstep with a huge bunch of flowers and a card apologising on behalf of his fellow Englishmen! As no one else knew of the incident I figured our names must have come up on the police computer and MI6 had been informed. It was a heart-warming gesture from a genuinely nice guy, but the knowledge that our everyday actions were being monitored in some small way helped instil a sense of security.

I certainly never abused my contacts with British Intelligence but it was comforting to know that I had access to them should the situation arise. In March 1995 Michelle and I booked a flight home but as the departure date drew near I began to get very cold feet and decided that it would be foolish to take the risk, particularly as we would be travelling with our one year-old daughter. As it happened, another close friend expressed an interest in taking up my ticket, but as you know, airlines won't change the name on a ticket once it has been issued. Well, it turns out they will if you know the right people… Having refused all our prior pleas to change the ticket, one phone call to James and it was done. As they say, it's not what you know but who you know.

I maintained regular contact with MI6 until 1996, when it began to tail off as the relevance of my information deteriorated with the passing of time. Obviously, the likelihood of any direct physical threat to me in the United Kingdom had long since passed. Nevertheless, I did have access to them, and from time to time they would make contact if they had a situation where I might be able to assist.

So, most of the time, I was Brian Morrow the teacher rather than Brian Morrow the spy. Still waters run deep, as the saying goes. It was really tough on both Michelle and me at times, particularly during the period between 1991 and 1994. I suppose that is why we felt so indebted to our contacts in British Intelligence. That was the only time we could let down our guard. The stress certainly built up over the years. The students I taught in that period would indeed be surprised to hear of the adventures of their 'normal' teacher!

This was also the time Michelle and I became parents. My first daughter was born in March 1994. In fact, by the mid-1990s we felt quite at home in the UK. Not only did we both have jobs, a house and a family, but the government had welcomed and supported us. Yet in 1995 I applied to return to South Africa.

Deep down there was never any real intent to return home. It was more a case of having the freedom to choose. There was a sense of frustration and some bitterness that I could not return, rather than any real desire to relocate permanently. In taking the documents, I had broken both the Official Secrets and the Protection of Information Acts, contravention of which carried a fine of R10 000, 10 years imprisonment or both. I felt that I needed some form of safeguard from the government if I was to go back to SA, even for a vacation, in order to negate any possible reprisals.

In this vein, I began making direct contact with the ANC in 1994 in an attempt to obtain indemnity for my 'illegal actions' and to obtain some sort of public acknowledgement of my actions, in order to provide a degree of protection from potential reprisals by my former Branch colleagues. My first point of contact was with Ronnie Press, an ANC official at the ANC 'offices' in London. Having outlined my circumstances, I was assured that the ANC would do all it could to assist me. Nothing happened. My sources in British Intelligence informed me that Press was a low-level ANC official and that to all intents and purposes I had been fobbed off.

I then decided to appeal directly to Nelson Mandela via his PA Jessie Duarte, but all I received was an email thanking me for making contact but pointing out that Mandela could not get involved in individual cases… I have to say, as arrogant as it may seem to some, that watching a succession of individuals parade through Nelson

Mandela's office, most notably the bloody Spice Girls, seeking an audience with the great man made my blood boil!

I appeared to be making better progress when I contacted Mike Sutcliffe, a name I knew well from the past as it had cropped up on numerous files in my time in 'White Organisations'. Sutcliffe, a prominent white anti-apartheid campaigner in the late 80s and 90s, had risen through the ranks of the ANC and was at this time an ANC MP in the KwaZulu-Natal Parliament. He appeared willing to help and agreed to meet my wife in Durban in July 1994 whilst she was in South Africa visiting her parents. After discussions with Michelle at the residence of my parents-in-law, Sutcliffe asked her to attend another meeting with Mo Shaik, an influential ANC operative (and brother of the now infamous Shabir) who had worked in the intelligence division of *Umkhonto we Sizwe*. This looked like a real breakthrough….

Michelle met with Shaik and Sutcliffe at a popular pub in Sherwood, Durban, where Shaik said that I was the just the type of person that the new South Africa needed and if I returned to the country I should have a role in the new administration. After receiving promises of assistance and assurances that they would be in contact, it came as no real surprise that we never heard from them again!

In 1995, I tried to use the media but to no avail. Although we made the front page in South Africa and the fifth page in the UK, I was informed that I could not be granted indemnity for my 'illegal' actions as my offence had been committed 'outside the timeframe'. Talk about being cheesed off! So convicted racist killers such as Barend Strydom could callously shoot eight blacks dead in the street and gain indemnity but, no, my actions fell outside the timeframe.

Andrew Baker, my new MI6 contact, suggested that I should change my name with the express purpose of using the assumed identity to enter South Africa without raising suspicion, slipping under the radar so to speak. I used the name Stuart Harris. I only ever assumed this pseudonym when travelling to and from South Africa.

It provided a solution and I was able to return a few times over the following years, but they could never be considered holidays in any sense of the word as I was obliged to keep a low profile and limit my activities considerably.

I usually returned to South Africa for personal reasons. In 1998, I went back for my father's funeral. On that visit, two incidents took place that highlighted the risks I was taking in returning to my homeland. Whilst working-out at the Westville gym in Durban I was pretty sure that I recognised a former operative, Warrant Officer Keith Brown, whom I knew from the SB as well as socially via the SAP football team. Unfortunately Keith had also identified me!

Keith was a fairly OK guy by Branch standards, but I was still pretty stressed to have been recognised. He came up to me and said 'I wouldn't think you would have come back to SA, Brian. People don't have many good things to say about you here.' I mentioned that I was on holiday and had no intention of returning to live. He said that we should meet up as he was interested in hearing my side of the story. I said that would be great and took his card, promising to be in touch in the near future. Now this was never going to happen as I knew full well that I was leaving in a couple of days.

The twist to the story occurred days later upon my return to the UK. My sister called and told me of an unusual incident that had taken place just after I left South Africa. A certain Graham Jordan had booked his car into my brother-in-law's garage for a service, a rather unusual occurrence as he had never made use of his premises before.

During a discussion, Jordan mentioned that he believed that he was my brother-in-law and that the rumour was that I had returned to South Africa. He asked my brother-in-law if he had seen me recently. Of course, my brother-in-law denied everything and nothing more was said.

Nevertheless, the implications were fairly sinister. Obviously, Keith Brown had mentioned our conversation to someone in the SAP, whether in passing or with malicious intent and it was abundantly clear that my actions had not been forgiven by die-hard ex-colleagues in the SB. Any return to South Africa carried the very real risk that I would be the target of an attack of some description and it was a chance that I was not prepared to take.

My last visit was in fact in 2001, and I have not been back since. I took one last chance to sneak back in. No gyms this time. By then I realised that my fate was sealed. I was always to be in exile… and then we moved to Australia.

This choice was made for the sake of the children. I have to say I emigrated to Australia somewhat reluctantly, but given my salary as a teacher, there was simply no way I could provide private schooling for their senior school education and condemning them to the comprehensive system simply wasn't an option! In addition, the remuneration afforded to teachers in Australia would allow me to provide a better lifestyle for my family.

I have a deep affinity for the UK, but life is somewhat of a struggle if you must live on average wages, particularly in wealthy areas such as the South East. House prices are now way beyond the reach of all but an affluent minority. Michelle, as well as sharing the above concerns, always found the weather difficult to come to terms with because the children had to spend a significant amount of time indoors.

I'm not sure if I will spend the rest of my life in Australia. The future is always difficult to predict, but ideally I would like to combine my teaching with greater involvement on the motivational speaking circuit. Over the past few years I have conducted presentations at a number of schools and universities (the most prestigious being Oxford and London Universities), outlining my experiences in the SAP and the ensuing Inkathagate scandal.

These talks have been extremely well received but work commitments and a lack of contacts in a new country have prevented me from expanding my interest in this area. Surprisingly, a number of Australian schools study apartheid or racism as part of their Year 10–12 syllabus, so there is a direct market niche, while schools such a Brisbane Grammar offer an ethics component where my experiences are reasonably appropriate. If the opportunity arose I would love to lecture at university, particularly if I could focus on South African history in the apartheid era.

It may seem somewhat arrogant to some that I always dreamt I would one day have a future in South African politics, but that seems destined to remain just a dream… While others like Lieutenant Gregory Rockman have been rewarded for their stand against apartheid with seats in Parliament, my actions have largely gone unheralded and unrewarded. In all honesty, whilst Rockman's revelations in highlighting the brutality of the SAP riot squads were laudable and his subsequent treatment unjust, his actions barely created a ripple of attention in contrast to Inkathagate, and in truth he wasn't telling anyone what they didn't already know…

Too many individuals in the ANC seem to consider the defeat of apartheid as an end in itself, which has led to one corrupt government replacing another without taking the needs of the population as a whole into account. Many seem content to enjoy the trappings of government rather than working to reduce the chronic imbalances in wealth and opportunity that remain in South African society.

Let's make it clear. Political ambition is not the reason for this book. Perhaps the major driving force behind the publication of this book is the manner in which the circumstances surrounding the scandal have been inaccurately presented by all the interested parties involved over the years. The press have created the impression that the exposé was the result of outstanding investigative journalism on their behalf. The reality is that the entire scandal was given to them on a plate and yet they still failed to use the information to its full potential. This illusion has been propagated in virtually every publication dealing with Inkathagate over the years, where these documents just materialised as if by magic.

The ANC are even more culpable. When I applied for indemnity in 1995, Maxwell Malaudzi, the then representative for the Minister of Safety and Security stated, 'Should he get preferential treatment because he leaked some documents?' Yeah, that's right Maxwell! They came free with a McDonald's burger and a tank of petrol! It is time to set the record straight. The ANC were more than willing to use the worldwide condemnation of the government for their own political advantage at the time, singing the praises of the 'brave individual' who had supplied the information, but when I sought assistance a few years later I was fobbed off.

Ultimately, this book is about recognition, perhaps even homecoming.

# Notes

1 For accounts of the Seven Days War see *The Seven Days War, 25–31 March 1990: The Victims' Narrative*, edited by John Aitchison. Pietermaritzburg: Centre for Adult Education University of Natal, 1991. ISBN 0-86980-806-0. See also *Faith in Turmoil: The Seven Days War*, edited by Lou Levine. Pietermaritzburg: PACSA, 1999. ISBN: ISBN 0-620-24324-4.

2 Quoted in *The Path to Democracy: A Background to the Constitutional Negotiations in South Africa*, by Davidson, A. & Per Strand. Uppsala: Uppsala University Press, 1993, p. 99.

3 Described by one secret police document as 'a project under the control of the South African police', UWUSA was formed in 1986, one year after the ANC-aligned Congress of South African Trade Unions (COSATU). It was supported by the American labour federation, AFL-CIO, which was a well-known conduit for American money to anti-communist groups.

4 *Appendix: The Third Force. TRC Report.* Volume 6, Section 4. http://www.info.gov.za/otherdocs/2003/trc/4_3ap.pdf

5 Confirmed by Gary Cullen, 13 October 2006.

6 Originally an Arabic term meaning 'unbeliever', in white South African culture it came to be the most offensive derogatory term used to refer to African people.

7 Literally 'salty penis'. A derogatory but not unamusing Afrikaner term to describe English-speaking white South African men who, because they had one leg planted in South Africa and one leg planted in Britain, would dangle their 'piels' in the sea.

# References


Aitchison, J. (ed.). *The Seven Days War, 25–31 March 1990: The Victims' Narrative*. Pietermaritzburg: Centre for Adult Education University of Natal, 1991.

Davidson, A.G and Per Strand. *The Path to Democracy: A Background to the Constitutional Negotiations in South Africa*. Uppsala: Uppsala University Press, 1993

Levine, L.(ed.). *Faith in Turmoil: The Seven Days War*. Pietermaritzburg: PACSA, 1999

# Glossary

*apartheid* – a system of racial segregation that was enforced in South Africa between 1948 and 1994. Under apartheid, people were legally classified according to their racial groups – mainly white, black, Indian and coloured – and were geographically, and forcibly, separated from one another on the basis of this classification.

*Askaris* – used to describe ANC guerrilla/terrorist fighters who had been 'persuaded' to change allegiance and work for the South African Police against their former comrades.

*braaivleis* – slang South African term for a barbeque. Literal translation would be 'burnt meat'.

*Caspir* – standard South African Police armoured riot vehicle.

*hostel* – massive residential area used to house single male Africans. They accommodated thousands of people.

*houtkop* – racist term used to describe the African population. Literal translation is 'wooden head'.

*kaffir* – the most common racist term used to describe blacks in the apartheid era.

*kaffirboetjie* – derogatory term for white South Africans who were considered to be sympathetic towards the plight of black South Africans.

*KwaMashu* – a black township/residential area on the northern outskirts of Durban.

*rooinek* – derogatory term for white South Africans of English descent. Developed from the observation that many whites with an English heritage tended to develop sunburn rather than tan. Literal translation is 'red neck'.

*safe house* – a residential/business abode not connected to intelligence services where sources could be briefed/debriefed without any obvious link to the authorities.

*soutpeel* – derogatory term for white South Africans of English descent; aimed at their alleged divided loyalties between South Africa and England. The inference was that they had one foot in England, the other in South Africa and their male appendage in the ocean in between. Literal translation is 'salt dick'.

*STRATCOM* – the intelligence term for the coordinated program of disinformation conducted by the SAP and various state intelligence agencies aimed at disrupting anti-apartheid opposition.

*Radio 702* – popular liberal Johannesburg radio station, often a voice of anti-government opinion in the late 1980s and early 1990s.

*Umlazi* – a black township on the southern outskirts of Durban.

*Youth Day* – commemorates the 16 June 1976 uprising in the black township of Soweto outside Johannesburg. Now a public holiday in South Africa.

*Vlakplaas* – notorious farm where many of the SAP Askaris were housed. It served as a base from where the so called 'death squads' could launch their attacks. The original Vlakplaas was under the command of Colonel Euguene de Kock. Every regional Security Branch had a 'farm' where their Askaris were housed.

# Index

## W



## Y